SO YOU REALLY WA
ARBITRA

DISPUTE RESOLUTION GUIDES

Practical Guide to Litigation
second edition
by Travers Smith Braithwaite
(1998)

What is Dispute Resolution?
by Dr Peter L. d'Ambrumenil
(1998)

Introduction to Arbitration
by Harold Crowter
(1998)

SO YOU REALLY WANT TO BE AN ARBITRATOR?

BY

D. MARK CATO
MSc (Construction Law & Arbitration), FRICS, FCIArb

LONDON HONG KONG
1999

LLP Reference Publishing
69–77 Paul Street
London EC2A 4LQ
Great Britain

EAST ASIA
LLP Asia
Sixth Floor, Hollywood Centre
233 Hollywood Road
Hong Kong

First published in Great Britain 1999

© D. Mark Cato, 1999

British Library Cataloguing in Publication Data
A catalogue record for this book is
available from the British Library

ISBN 1-85978-879-3

All rights reserved. No part of this publication may be reproduced, stored in a retrieval system, or transmitted, in any form or by any means, electronic, mechanical, photocopying, recording or otherwise, without the prior written permission of
LLP Limited

Whilst every effort has been made to ensure that the information contained in this book is correct neither the editors and contributors nor LLP Limited can accept any responsibility for any errors or omissions or for any consequences resulting therefrom.

Are you satisfied with our customer service?

These telephone numbers are your service hot lines for questions and queries:

Delivery: +44 (0) 1206 772866
Payment/invoices/renewals: +44 (0) 1206 772114
LLP Products & Services: +44 (0) 1206 772113
e-mail: Publications@LLPLimited.com or fax us on +44 (0) 1206 772771

We welcome your views and comments in order to ease any problems and answer any queries you may have.

LLP Limited, Colchester CO3 3LP, U.K.

Text set in 10/12pt Plantin by
Selwood Systems, Midsomer Norton
Printed in Great Britain by
WBC Limited,
Bridgend, Mid-Glamorgan

*This book is dedicated to The Young:
my dearest son and daughter
Miles & Chloe*

FOREWORD

BY THE RIGHT HONOURABLE
THE LORD SAVILLE OF NEWDIGATE[1]

Arbitration is a form of alternative dispute resolution, that is to say an alternative to resolving disputes through the courts. It depends on the agreement of the parties to a dispute to use a private tribunal to decide on their rights and obligations. Under our law, the decision of the arbitral tribunal is binding on the parties and there are very limited means indeed of recourse to the courts if one or other of the parties is dissatisfied with the conduct of the arbitration or the result reached by the arbitral tribunal. The reason for this is that since the parties have agreed to arbitrate their disputes, it would be wrong for the law (save in the most exceptional of circumstances) to allow one or other of them to seek to substitute the decision of the court for the decision of the arbitral tribunal. To do otherwise would in effect be to allow one or other of the parties unilaterally to tear up the bargain they have made to seek a private resolution of their dispute.

In these circumstances, arbitrators bear a heavy responsibility; both in the way they conduct arbitrations and in reaching their decision on the dispute they have agreed to resolve, since it is most unlikely that the courts will interfere. Like judges, they must seek to ensure that justice is not only done but is also seen to be done. Part of this task involves adapting procedures suitable for the case in question, always remembering that unnecessary delay and expense itself causes injustice.

---

1. Chairman of the Departmental Advisory Committee on Arbitration Law; as successor to Lord Mustill he could be said to be the "architect" of the Arbitration Act 1996.

viii Foreword

The Arbitration Act 1996 sets out in ordinary English the basic powers and duties of arbitrators and the general principles to apply. However, since a particular strength of arbitration lies in its ability to tailor resolution procedures to the particular dispute in question, the Act did not seek to go further. Indeed, any attempt to do so would have been misguided, since appropriate procedures change with the type of dispute in question and indeed change as time goes by, so that a fixed statutory code of procedure would have rendered inflexible this most desirable flexibility.

This means that experienced arbitrators have much to teach those who want to become arbitrators. Turning theory into practice in any walk of life is difficult, if not impossible, without guidance from those who have actually done the job.

This book helps to provide that guidance. The author is someone who combines great practical knowledge as an arbitrator with the ability to write simply and clearly. He has provided an invaluable source of information on how actually to conduct arbitrations. Although in his Preface the author describes the work as being designed for the early studies of would-be arbitrators, to my mind many arbitrators already practising would also be able to learn much of value from the wise and practical advice to be found in these pages.

October 1998   MARK SAVILLE

PREFACE

This book should appeal to those who believe that they would like to become arbitrators but need to know more about the process before finally committing themselves, and, once having done so, the subject-matter is written in sufficient depth to carry them through the early stages of their studies. Taking the reader through from A to Z of the process, it contains sufficient information and advice to carry a tyro through his or her first arbitration, provided it is a relatively simple dispute. There is also a short section on adjudication at the very end, which, although it is not arbitration, deserves a mention when discussing dispute resolution, particularly in the light of the recent legislation—my thanks to my friend and colleague John Riches for this contribution.

Writing the book as a conversation between me and my god-daughter, Thomasina, who has decided that she wants to study to become an arbitrator, enabled me, as author, to prompt her to ask the sorts of questions which all students would like to ask but fail to because they erroneously feel that they should know the answer without asking.

Thomasina has a boyfriend, Charley (Pilkington-Smythe). Charley conveniently happens to be a pupil of a rent review arbitrator and he joins us from time to time through the several sessions that I have with Thomasina and, when he does, the conversation inevitably ends up with Charley telling us the differences between what we have been discussing and the way they do things in the rent review world—very different, but equally valid.

As I illustrate the discussions with documentation—both mine, as a construction arbitrator, and Charley's—relevant to the part of the process that we happen to be discussing at the time, the reader is given a rare insight into the inner workings of experienced practising arbitrators.

x Preface

The text is also splattered with practical advice and tips garnered from my experience in over 100 references in which I have been appointed arbitrator—some big and some very small, but each case in its own way equally demanding.

For example, although it may be a case where there is a small amount at stake, the outcome may well determine the financial survival of one, or even both, disputants. For this reason all the niceties have to be observed, no matter what the size of the case or whether the parties are representing themselves or have instructed solicitors and barristers. But having said that, "horses for courses", the arbitrator has a duty to adopt procedures suitable to the case and as such must demonstrate a flexibility of approach.

Although I have illustrated some procedures by reference to specific documents used in construction disputes, this book is written to appeal to all arbitral disciplines, many of which have their own Rules, so if it is not a construction or rent review case, it is a question of applying the Rules (if any) applicable to that discipline.

Do not be fooled by the reader-friendly nature of the conversational text—this is a serious book and will certainly reward the assiduous reader by arming him or her with a first-class working knowledge of the arbitral process. It is for this reader that the text is discreetly annotated throughout with references to the relevant sections of the Arbitration Act 1996. Thus this serious reader will be able to pursue his or her studies to the next level by reading the Act for themselves in conjunction with the relevant passage of the text where the reference to a particular section appears.

Read and enjoy.

Clavering, October 1998   D. MARK CATO

ABOUT THE AUTHOR

D. Mark Cato is a Chartered Surveyor and has worked in many countries of the world, including the USA, Australia, France, Italy, the Southern Republic of the Yemen, Bahrain and throughout the Persian Gulf, Ethiopia and Somalia.

Since the late 1980s he has been a full-time arbitrator and has been appointed in around 100 references. He lectures at various universities and speaks regularly at seminars and conferences on arbitration in the UK and overseas.

He is a well-known author on arbitration with three major works to his name: *Arbitration Practice and Procedure—Interlocutory and Hearing Problems (Second Edition)*; *The Sanctuary House Case—An Arbitration Workbook* and the forthcoming *The Expert in Litigation and Arbitration*.

He is a Registered Arbitrator and at date of publication is a member of the General Council, member of the Executive Board and Chairman of the Professional Committee of the Chartered Institute of Arbitrators. He took an internal Masters degree in Construction Law and Arbitration at King's College, London in 1993.

He is the Founder President of the Arbitration Club, which, together with its off-shoot, The International Arbitration Club, has over 400 members in seven branches.

He is married with two grown-up children and lives with Alice, his wife, on the Herts/Essex border. In October 1998 he became the proud grandfather of little Freddy.

CONTENTS

	Page
Foreword	vii
Preface	ix
About the Author	xi

CHAPTER 1.	INTRODUCTION	1
CHAPTER 2.	HISTORICAL	3
CHAPTER 3.	WHAT IS ARBITRATION?	5

Source of power and authority	6
Arbitration agreement—before and after dispute has arisen	10
Appointment	11
Tribunal of more than one arbitrator	16
Advantages of arbitration	17

CHAPTER 4.	THE ARBITRATOR'S OPENING SHOT	19

Letter following appointment	20

CHAPTER 5.	THE PRELIMINARY MEETING	31

The agenda		33
Discussion on agenda		50
Item 1.00	Introduction	50
Item 2.00	Appointment	50
Item 3.00	Jurisdiction	51
Item 4.00	Seat and applicable law	52

Contents

Item 5.00	Commencement of the arbitration	52
Item 6.00	Identifying items in dispute	53
Item 7.00	Arbitrator's general powers	55
Items 7.01.1–4		56
Item 7.01.5	Whether and to what extent the tribunal should itself take the initiative in ascertaining the facts and the law	56
Item 7.01.6	Whether and to what extent there should be oral or written evidence or submissions	56
Item 7.01.7	The award of interest	57
Item 7.02		57
Item 7.02.2	Power to make a declaratory award	58
Item 7.02.3	Powers in case of a party's default	58
Item 7.02.4	Power to record the parties' agreement	58
Item 7.03	The arbitrator shall have power ...	58
Item 7.03.1	Power to appoint an expert	58
Item 7.03.2	Power to order a party to do or refrain from doing anything	59
Item 7.03.3	Power to order specific performance	59
Item 7.03.4	Power to order rectification of a deed or document	59
Item 7.03.5	Power to order provisional relief	60
Item 8.00	Joinder/consolidation	61
Item 9.00	Issues	61
Item 10.00	Proceedings	61
Item 10.01	Documents only	62
Item 10.02	Short procedure with a hearing	63
Item 10.03	A full procedure with a hearing	63
Item 10.03.1	Scott Schedule	64
Item 10.03.2	Timetable	64
Item 10.03.2.7	No provision for further and better particulars	65
Item 10.03.3	Witness statements	65
Item 10.03.4	Experts	66
Item 10.03.5	Disclosure of documents	67
Item 10.03.6	General	68
Item 10.03.6.4	Offers	68
Item 10.03.7	Pre-hearing review	69
Item 10.03.8	Hearing	69
Item 10.03.8.3	Venue/accommodation	70
Item 10.03.8.4	Hearing bundle	70
Item 10.03.8.5	Rules of evidence	71
Item 10.03.8.6	Evidence under oath	71
Item 10.03.8.7	Limitation on orality	72

Item 10.03.8.8 Text books/law reports	72
Item 10.03.9 Advocates' submissions	73
Item 11.00 Representation	73
Item 12.00 Reasoned award	74
Item 13.00 Exclusion agreement	76
Item 14.00 Costs	77
Item 14.01 Security for costs	77
Item 14.02 Recoverable costs	77
Item 15.00 Inspection	78
Item 16.00 Agreement on common ground	78
Item 17.00 Arbitrator's terms and conditions	79
Item 18.00 Insurance	86
Item 19.00 Any other business	87
Order for directions	89
Discussion on order for directions	99
Item 1.00 Parties	99
Item 2.00 Appointments	99
Item 3.00 Jurisdiction	100
Item 7.00 Arbitrator's general powers	100
Item 11.00 Service	100
Item 22.00 Costs	101
Items 26.00–28.00 Further directions	101

CHAPTER 6. RENT REVIEW ARBITRATIONS 103

Model letter	104
Direction for preliminary meeting	108
Agenda for preliminary meeting	114
Pleadings	116
Order for Directions on "documents only" after a Preliminary Meeting	119
Appointments—nominated or consensual	122
Oral hearing or "documents only"?	122
Pleadings or Statement of Case?	125
Advantages	126
Disadvantages	126
Differences between Statements of Case and Formal Pleadings	127
Advantages of the Statement of Case procedure over Formal Pleadings	128
Disadvantages of the Statement of Case procedure	128
Defences	129
The arbitrator's duty in rent review disputes	130
The process of reasoning in rent review cases	130

xvi Contents

Procedural problems in rent review arbitrations	131
Constructional issues	132
Admissibility of evidence	132
Evaluating opinion evidence	134
Reasons in rent review dispute awards	135

CHAPTER 7. WHAT IS THIS INTERLOCUTORY PERIOD?	139
General	139
What sort of interlocutory directions?	140
Further and better particulars	143
Disadvantages	145
Failure to comply with direction for further and better particulars	146
Unless Order in respect of failure to reply to further and better particulars	147
Alternatives to further and better particulars	149
Notices to Admit Facts and Interrogatories	149
Typical order re Notice to Admit Facts	151
Typical Request for Interrogatories (questions from the arbitrator)	156
Security for costs application	157
Typical direction for procedure for dealing with security for costs application	160
Discovery	163
Extensions of time	164
Generally failing to comply with the arbitrator's directions	164
Ex parte proceedings	165
Awards on different issues and partial awards	166
Pre-hearing review	167

CHAPTER 8. MORE ON THE ARBITRATOR	169
Adversarial or inquisitorial process?	169
Use of own expertise	172
Arbitrator—resignation or termination	173
Resignation	173
Termination	174
Immunity of arbitrator	174
Fees and how to get them paid	175

CHAPTER 9. THE COURT'S ROLE IN ARBITRAL PROCEEDINGS	177

	Contents	xvii
CHAPTER 10.	THE HEARING	181

CHAPTER 11.	WET TOWEL TIME—WRITING THE AWARD	187

Flow chart showing how to analyse a point of claim or counterclaim 189
The drafting of the award 190
The essentials of a valid award 190
The structure and content of the award 191
Example of a rent review award final as to all matters except costs of the arbitration 196

CHAPTER 12.	COSTS	201

What costs? 202

CHAPTER 13.	AGREED AWARD ON SETTLEMENT	205

CHAPTER 14.	POST-AWARD	207

Correcting errors in the award 207
Determination of the parties' costs 208
Appeals to the court 209

CHAPTER 15.	OTHER FORMS OF DISPUTE RESOLUTION	211

Alternative dispute resolution (ADR) 211
Capitulation 212
Negotiation 213
Mediation/conciliation 213
   Disadvantages of mediation/conciliation 214
Adjudication 215

Index 221

CHAPTER 1

INTRODUCTION

A god-daughter of mine, Thomasina, is a rising star in the City (of London). I believe she works for an international bank or finance company—she is certainly involved in commercial contracts both in the UK and abroad.

One day Thomasina came to see me and asked about arbitration.

She said that all of their contracts included a clause referring any dispute arising out of, or in connection with, that contract to arbitration and she really would like to know more about the process. I suspect that the fact that her boyfriend, Charley (Pilkington-Smythe), who works for one of those smart West End firms of surveyors and is a rent review arbitrator's pupil—a "rent boy", as it is known in the trade—may also have something to do with her sudden enthusiasm!

However, not to be too cynical about her motives, she told me that a dispute had arisen recently on a domestic contract with which she was involved and, although she was only on the fringes of the action, it had whetted her interest as she could see the possibility of acting herself as the arbitrator, in such a dispute. At some stage in the future, of course, she added with a sheepish grin, not wishing to belittle my advanced years. Anyway, she came to ask me, as a seasoned arbitrator, whether this was a realistic objective; but first, she said, she would appreciate an in-depth discussion of what arbitration was all about and how it worked in practice.

As the dear girl's godfather, I had been called upon to do little more, over the years, than to cough up for birthdays and Christmases and attend the odd performance at school of such delights as Aristophanes' *The Frogs* (in ancient Greek!) or some concert or other. I felt the least that I could do was to devote a little time to encouraging the bright young thing to join the serried ranks of arbitrators.

Of course, I agreed but warned that it would not be a five-minute chat. If she really wanted an in-depth discussion she could have it, but we certainly would not finish today. She accepted my caution with alacrity. So where to begin?

CHAPTER 2

HISTORICAL

Suffice it to say that arbitration is as old as trade itself. For our purpose, I explained, arbitration as a means of resolving trade disputes flourished in Britain certainly as early as Roman times and came into its own with the founding of the Courts of Pie Powder in the fifteenth century (a corruption of the Norman French *pieds poudrés*—Dusty Feet—so named as it is said that the dispute was resolved before the litigants had time to shake the dust from their feet). These courts were presided over by law merchants where the emphasis was on speed, simplicity of procedure, and, more importantly, privacy, all of which we are attempting to return to today.

As the doyen of arbitration, Lord Mustill, said in his opus on the subject:

"It has been recognised for centuries that commercial men prefer to use arbitration rather than the courts to resolve business disputes."

Why should that be? Broadly speaking because the perceived advantage of arbitration over litigation is just what those dusty merchants offered, privacy and flexibility of procedure. At least, flexibility of procedure, while having been available to the arbitrator, was not always used to advantage, and for a period arbitration fell into disrepute—indeed until quite recently—because, perhaps, of the increasing involvement of lawyers. It became little more than litigation without wigs. Some say, not entirely fairly in my view, that the process was hijacked by lawyers.

All of that has now changed, at least potentially, I told Thomasina, with the enactment of the Arbitration Act 1996—but more of that later.

CHAPTER 3

WHAT IS ARBITRATION?

Before we got into a detailed discussion of the procedures that are followed in arbitration, I asked Thomasina what she thought arbitration was. She suggested that it was a means of getting people together and trying to thrash out a solution to a dispute. She mentioned ACAS—the Arbitration and Conciliation Service, which is frequently used when there are disputes between employers and their workforce. I had to disenchant her and say that ACAS had very little, if anything, to do with arbitration, despite its name. It is, in fact, a pure mediation service.

When we had completed our consideration of arbitration I promised her that I would touch on the current vogue for ADR (alternative dispute resolution) as an alternative to arbitration, which includes mediation, and is currently enjoying some limited success.

To be fair to Thomasina, her description of arbitration was not far off the mark.

One definition I was given, as a student, was as follows:

"The private reference of a dispute or difference between two or more parties for a determination, after consideration of the evidence adduced and arguments of all parties, by a person or persons, validly appointed, acting judicially."

Well, she said, if that is arbitration, it sounds pretty similar to litigation to me; with things like adducing evidence, argument and acting judicially. Inasmuch as an arbitrator must act fairly between the parties, giving each an opportunity of presenting its case and answering the case made against it, I told Thomasina that she was right. The arbitrator, in that respect, is like a judge. He makes his determination, as opposed to delivering a judgment (usually in the form of a written Award) based on the evidence, or, if you prefer it, based on the submissions made to him by the parties. The form which these submissions can take we will explore a little later when we look at the alternative procedures discussed during the preliminary meeting.

So far so good, she said. I understand that arbitration is a process, presided over by an individual, in private, who hears what the parties have to say about their dispute and then comes to a decision, based on what they have said, or have set down on paper, which decision he then communicates to the parties.

But where does this arbitrator's power come from; how is he chosen; what if one party wants one arbitrator and the other party prefers somebody else; what happens once he has made his determination? You say it is usually set out in writing; how it is to be enforced? Her questions came out in a rush. Clearly, she was going to be a receptive pupil.

Hold you hard, as they say in Norfolk, one step at a time, I said. So many questions, all perfectly reasonable, but let us not run before we can walk. The best way I can illustrate many of the points that you have raised is to go through a fairly standard agenda for the meeting, which usually—and I stress *usually*, as this is not an invariable practice in all forms of arbitration—takes place at the commencement of the dispute, between the arbitrator and the parties. However, before we look at this agenda, I will just say this about the arbitrator's powers and his authority.

SOURCE OF POWER AND AUTHORITY

Quite simply, the arbitrator's power comes from the parties through a number of different sources—initially through the arbitration agreement, which can be incorporated into a contract such as those that Thomasina herself uses in commercial transactions. In such a case the clause would speak of referring disputes and differences between the parties to arbitration.

Most such arbitration clauses say a little more than that, although the two words "Arbitration London" have been held, in court, to be a valid arbitration clause. Most arbitration clauses are far more detailed, and some go so far as to spell out the procedures to be followed by the arbitrator in conducting the arbitration. This can either form part of the arbitration clause itself or, as often happens in standard contracts (such as the family of construction contracts, the JCT forms) through reference to published procedural rules (in the case of construction contracts, the JCT Arbitration Rules, the ICE Arbitration Procedure or, more recently, the CIMA Rules (designed to cover the whole of the construction industry)). We shall look at such rules in more detail when we come to consider my standard agenda, I told her.

At this stage, I warned the dear girl that many of the points that I would be discussing or illustrating in attempting to summarise the arbitral process would inevitably relate to construction and property matters. That, after all, was my field and the one I knew most about. Having said that, I emphasised that there were many other forms of arbitration, apart from construction. Possibly—almost certainly—the most popular and widely-used concerned rent reviews of commercial properties, I said. Although the numbers of referrals had fallen off considerably over the past few years, as inflation had dropped dramatically and rents had stabilised, there were still something in the region of 8,000 references a year, to be decided either by arbitration or expert determination.

The next, possibly most widely-used, field of arbitration exists in the maritime world. Indeed, much of our arbitral law has derived from maritime cases. As she was a well-educated girl there was no need for me to point out to Thomasina that, as we are a seafaring nation trading with all corners of the earth, disputes between shippers, the shipowners and the merchant venturers *et al.*, had been around for a very long time.

However, I have been diverted from the point I was making about the source of the arbitrator's power and authority, I said. Apart from the arbitration agreement itself, another source of power is the submission which the parties (or quite often the claimant by unilateral application) make to the arbitrator when he is first approached to deal with the dispute—in other words, what the parties ask him to resolve will limit his jurisdiction.

I apologised to Thomasina for using the legal expression *jurisdiction*, for, make no mistake, I told her, that is what it is in this context, as it has a very significant impact of the whole process of arbitration, and, like it or not, I would have to expand on this expression as we went through our discussion.

As the parties can inadvertently limit the arbitrator's jurisdiction

8 What is arbitration?

in the manner of their approach to him in the first instance, it is also possible for them expressly to limit his jurisdiction by agreement, I told her. Although this point strictly touches more on jurisdiction than on source of power, a limit on jurisdiction is certainly a limitation of the arbitrator's power which must not be exceeded. If it is there can be dire consequences for both arbitrator and parties.

The third, and possibly the most important, source of power is Acts of Parliament (statutes) and common law. We are very fortunate in this country, as I mentioned previously, that quite recently (30 January 1997) a new "user-friendly" Arbitration Act (AA '96) was brought into force.

Why was this so important? Thomasina asked. Surely it's an informal process that does not require statute law at all? I referred her again to the definition of arbitration and the requirement for the arbitrator to act judicially. If you define judicially as "*in the manner of a judge*", I said, then you will realise that there must be *some* basic rules laid down. This does not mean that the arbitrator is bound by the same rules and regulations as a judge (such as, for example, in the UK High Court, the *White Book*, or, as it is commonly called, the RSC—the *Rules of the Supreme Court*); but, while not being as constrained as a judge, the arbitrator is bound by certain conventions and protocol. If there is a written arbitration clause, then the Arbitration Act can apply—indeed it is a prerequisite under the Act that the arbitration agreement be in writing for the Act to apply.

A number of the sections of this AA '96 are mandatory, and therefore the parties are bound by them. Many other sections are open to the parties to agree or disagree on alternative procedures. Fundamentally, in the absence of agreement—and the parties frequently find it difficult to even agree on the time of day—the arbitrator is free to decide procedural and evidential matters (s.34 AA '96).

Oh dear, Thomasina said, you're already getting heavy and starting to mention sections of this Act. All I really wanted was a general description of arbitration. I told her that I made no apology for deliberately mentioning the part of the Act by its section number, as there were half a dozen or so such sections, of which anyone the slightest bit interested in arbitration, or at least contemplating becoming an arbitrator, must be aware.

So, I said. I shall mention just a few of the key sections of this

Act as we go through because they can have an important influence on the way in which the arbitrator and the parties conduct themselves and the reference. Incidentally, I explained that the word *reference* is no longer used in the current Act. However, I continue to use it as I believe that it is suitably descriptive of the process of referring a dispute to the determination of a third person.

Having said that, Thomasina was relieved to learn that I did not intend to go through these key sections of the Act at this particular point in time, but would defer doing so until we discussed the agenda for the Preliminary Meeting, to which I referred earlier.

Apart from statute law, Thomasina asked, where does the common law come in? I explained that, so far as the law is concerned, the arbitrator is bound by the authority of decided cases, at least those of the higher courts: the High Court, the Court of Appeal and the House of Lords, in that order of precedence. If he gets the law so badly wrong that it substantially affects the outcome of the dispute he has been appointed to determine, this can be one of the grounds for appeal, as we will see later.

Does this mean that arbitrators need to be lawyers or have a sound knowledge of the law? she asked. I retorted that where complex legal points were involved in disputes the parties usually engage the services of lawyers who will explain the law to the arbitrator, or at least their view of it. With lawyers on both sides the arbitrator will frequently be presented with two different interpretations of the law, so that it is for him to determine which of the two interpretations presented to him he believes is most applicable to the facts of the case that he is hearing.

Having said that, there is provision in the AA '96 for the parties to agree that the arbitrator acts *ex aequo et bono*, which I understand literally means *by way of equality and goodness* or, in simple language, that the arbitrator is not bound to decide the dispute in accordance with any formal system of law at all. For example, he would be permitted to apply the general sense of what is fair and just, rather than strict legal rules. A sort of wisdom of Solomon? said Thomasina questioningly. Not quite, I said. The arbitrator still has to act judicially and I am not sure that cutting the baby in half, or even threatening to, would pass muster.

It has been said that, subject to three limitations, there is an assumption that an arbitrator will have such powers as are necessary for the discharge of his obligations. These three limitations are:

10 What is arbitration?

1. Public policy;
2. No jurisdiction over third parties;
3. No transfer of rights reserved by the courts.

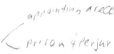

The first of these speaks for itself. Clearly nothing decided by the arbitrator or procedure adopted by him, can be against public policy. He could not, for example, direct a party to engage in an illegal activity.

The second point, concerning jurisdiction over third parties, of course could be said to be one of the drawbacks of arbitration when compared with litigation. However, as will be seen, I said, there are, under certain circumstances, powers of joinder, i.e. in the ability to join third parties, and/or consolidate actions. Consolidation is combining more than one reference, where the parties to those separate disputes are common to both and the substantive issue is also common to both. Never fear, I said, this is a complex issue and we will be looking at this aspect of arbitration in a little more detail where we get to that item on the agenda.

The third point concerns certain powers which only the court can exercise in support of arbitral proceedings. Two such are the appointment of a receiver and committing a party to prison for perjury. These powers are exclusively reserved to the court and cannot be transferred to an arbitrator.

ARBITRATION AGREEMENT—BEFORE AND AFTER DISPUTE HAS ARISEN

When you start talking about the arbitrator's source of power, Thomasina said, you said that one source was the arbitration agreement. Yes, I said, such an agreement is usually found in contracts, and invariably so in standard contracts, but it can be as simple as an exchange of letters.

What happens if there is no arbitration agreement and the parties decided that they would like their dispute settled by arbitration? she asked. For example, a row over holiday which did not match the description in the brochure? Well, I said, you happen to have chosen an example where disputes, certainly those involving ABTA, are covered by a clause in the holiday contract, referring them to arbitration. But, quite simply, if parties have no such agreement and wish to arbitrate, they merely enter into an *ad hoc* agreement. Entered into after the dispute has arisen, they can even agree that one party or the other pays all of the costs, but they cannot make that provision before the dispute arises.

Finally, before we got involved in going through the agenda for the Preliminary Meeting, Thomasina asked how does the arbitrator come to be appointed in the first place? Do the parties choose him or is he imposed upon them?

APPOINTMENT

I explained that there are a number of ways in which the arbitrator can be appointed. By far the best way is for the parties themselves to agree on someone of whom they have had experience and therefore in whom they have confidence. This is easiest where solicitors are involved, for they may be familiar with the body of arbitrators in their particular discipline. There are, of course, some client bodies, such as major building firms, who by the very nature of their business find themselves involved in disputes between themselves and the building employer or themselves and their subcontractors, and as such have a good knowledge of the few first-class arbitrators there are in the construction industry.

In these cases, then, when they find themselves in dispute, they can, and indeed should, attempt to agree with the other party on the name of someone in whom both have confidence—sadly this very rarely occurs. The claimant, having proposed one of, say, several names to the respondent, will frequently find them all rejected as the suspicion lurks that they are all friends of the claimant.

Of course, this is rarely, if ever, the case, but unfortunately that is the perception. In these circumstances the respondent usually replies with names of his own, all of which are also rejected for the same reason, as he was not prepared to accept any of the claimant's nominees. Having reached this impasse, most well-drawn arbitration clauses—and certainly those in the JCT family of building contracts—make provision for an appointment to be made by a third party in the event that the parties cannot themselves agree. Depending upon the contract or the standard form this can be the President or a vice-president of the Royal Institution of Chartered

Surveyors, the President of the Royal Institute of British Architects or, in the case of non-building disputes, the Chairman of the Chartered Institute of Arbitrators, the President of the Law Society or the Chairman of the Bar Council *et al.*

The main thing to remember about all of these appointments is that the selected arbitrator should have no connection with either party which could leave him open to an accusation of bias or partiality. Any connection, even with the party's advisers, if such are known at the time the arbitrator is approached, should be disclosed, otherwise the arbitrator leaves himself open to a subsequent challenge and possible removal.

I recalled one personal experience of this when a very large firm of City solicitors was appointed to advise a claimant in an arbitration in which I was the arbitrator. One of the partners in that firm was a very good friend of mine who had assisted me in writing one of my books. The partner allocated to that arbitration was not known to me. I made no mention, at the preliminary meeting, of my friendship with the other partner. Substantially through the reference the respondent somehow got wind of my friendship with this other partner and raised it as a possible ground for having me removed, for what was called in those days *misconduct*. Fortunately, I was able to persuade him that there was no firm ground for doing so, but it proved to be a good object lesson.

The most famous, or perhaps infamous, example I can recall was where an arbitrator was removed for partiality where it was discovered that the wife of one of the parties was his mistress and had been before he was appointed!

I should have mentioned earlier, I said, that the essence of arbitration is that the chosen arbitrator is an expert in the field in which the dispute has arisen. For example, if the dispute involves a *charterparty* (that is what a contract between shipowners and charterers is called), then the arbitrator—or in maritime cases frequently two arbitrators and an umpire—will be chosen from the shipping world.

Similarly, if a landlord and tenant cannot agree on the level of rent review the matter would probably be referred to the arbitration of a Chartered Surveyor experienced in the letting of properties or rent reviews with a specialist knowledge of the area in which the property subject to the review is located.

Does this mean then, asked Thomasina, that where such a expert is involved, he can use his expert knowledge to assist him to decide which of the parties to the dispute he will find for?

Yes, I said, that can be the case where the person is appointed as an independent expert and not as an arbitrator. Having said that, I told her that I did not want to complicate matters at this stage by going into detail about the differences between arbitration and expert determination, so we must assume for the moment that the expert has been appointed as an arbitrator. This means that he must observe what are often called the rules of natural justice. These are simply summarised as follows, I said, showing off my knowledge of Latin!

> *Nemo judex in causa sua:* nobody is to be judge in his own cause
> and
> *Audi alteram partem:* hear the other side—give the parties a fair hearing.

(If these are the rules of natural justice, what are the rules of unnatural justice? Lord Mustill asks.)

Forget that last flippant remark, I said, returning to the arbitrator. It is on these submissions from the parties that the arbitrator makes his determination, but there is no reason why he should not use his special expertise, for which he was chosen, to try this dispute, provided he tells the parties what is in his mind and gives each of them the opportunity of considering it and addressing him on it.

Appointing bodies, such as the Royal Institution of Chartered Surveyors (RICS), when they are considering making an appointment, ask the prospective appointee to confirm that the dispute falls within the sphere of his experience. Without such confirmation that person is unlikely to be appointed.

This seemed a perfect moment to explain to Thomasina the difference between arbitrators who are appointed by a third party and then communicate that appointment to the parties and those who approach the parties, for example to agree their terms and conditions, before they accept the appointment.

The first category, typically comprising arbitrators appointed by the RICS, arises following an application to the appointing body—usually from the claimant—where the parties themselves have failed to agree on an arbitrator. The President (or more likely his staff) will contact one or more prospective arbitrators to ensure their availability and expertise to deal with the particular dispute for

14 What is arbitration?

which he is being asked to appoint a arbitrator. Having received the necessary assurances, the President will then make the appointment; in other words, sign the appointing document and send that to the now arbitrator. That arbitrator will then communicate his appointment to the parties, invariably by letter.

Do you mean to say that this is the first time that the parties have learned the name of the person who has been appointed to oversee their dispute? asked Thomasina. Yes, I said, with an RICS appointment, that's exactly what happens.

But what about their fees and conditions? Don't they have to agree these with the parties before they accept the appointment? she asked. What if they consider that the arbitrator's fees are too high, or they don't like some of his terms? Surely they must have the opportunity of rejecting him?

Of course, you are right, I agreed. That is the normal way. Most appointments are made following agreement of the arbitrator's terms and conditions with the parties. The arbitrator, or rather the prospective arbitrator, contacts the parties with a copy of his terms and conditions, asking them to agree these before he accepts the appointment. The signature of both parties to these terms can crystallise the appointment or, alternatively, the arbitrator can write to the parties, on receipt of the signed terms, and say that he now accepts the appointment.

In the case of the RICS, as I say, the arbitrator is appointed before agreement of his fees and conditions—indeed most of my appointments have come that way, I told her. Rarely is it a problem, as I shall explain later. All that happens is that, following the appointment, I send the parties a copy of my terms and invite them to sign and return them to me. In the majority of cases they are returned signed. However where, in the odd instance, one party or the other—usually the respondent, who is not particularly interested in pursuing the arbitrator, for obvious reasons—refuses to sign the terms I do not press him, but leave the matter to be discussed at the preliminary meeting—as you will see later, I told her.

I suggested that we leave this particular issue, at this stage. We will certainly return to it later when we consider the arbitrator's fees and such emotive issues as his cancellation charges.

Fees aside, I suggested that, although I did not want to get too deep into the law, I felt that it would be sensible to touch on some of the problems that can arise over appointments. After all, it must be obvious to you, I said, that if you don't get the appointment right, the arbitration is doomed from the beginning.

Thomasina agreed that that sounded logical.

Why don't the parties interview prospective arbitrators before they choose one? Thomasina said. What a bright girl you are, I told her. This is a particular hobby-horse of mine. I absolutely agree, an interview can be a very effective selection process. At least that way the parties would get someone of their own choice and would not be foisted with an arbitrator who might not be particularly competent.

However, a warning, I said. If you ever find yourself in this position in the future, only attend an interview with representatives of both parties present. This is in pursuance of one of the golden rules of arbitration—that you do not communicate, at any time, with one party alone. Obviously, to do so could lead to the suspicion that you have heard something from the party from whom you received the communication, which might influence your decision in their favour and on which the other party has not had the opportunity of addressing you.

Right, said Thomasina, so much for interviews, what about these invalid appointments that you spoke about? Well, I said, the sort of thing that can happen is that, where there are alternative appointing bodies named in, say, pre-printed standard contracts, when the parties come to enter into that contract they might delete one or other of these alternatives. For example, in a building contract the parties may be offered a choice of appointing bodies from either the President of the RICS or the President of the RIBA. They delete the first option, but when a dispute arises, the claimant, making a unilateral application, overlooks this deletion and makes his application to the RICS, instead of to the RIBA, which subsequently makes the appointment.

So where does that leave the poor old arbitrator? asked Thomasina. Well, I said, I have actually been in that position myself. In a case like that the appointment would be invalid and any directions that the arbitrator gave would have no legal force. That would be the position where the invalidity arose through an innocent act or omission of one of the parties. But where the party applying for the appointment knew of the invalidity, it would almost certainly be estopped by waiver if it then proceeded to take a step in the proceedings. Rather like jurisdiction, which we shall discuss later,

16 What is arbitration?

any objection, for example to an arbitrator's appointment, must be made timeously. Of course, an innocent simple oversight could easily be remedied by an agreement between the parties. Alternatively, if, as often happens, there is a reluctant respondent who has not the slightest interest in getting involved in an arbitration and therefore refuses to co-operate to correct this innocent error, there again there is an easy remedy available to the claimant. He merely makes a fresh application to the correct appointing body.

Another form of invalid appointment can arise where the arbitration agreement itself specifies an arbitrator with particular qualifications—for example, one with at least 10 years' experience on the Baltic Exchange, for a commodity dispute, or, in the case of a maritime dispute, that the arbitrator must be a member of the LMAA. These are perfectly reasonable requirements in cases such as these, for to appoint even an experienced arbitrator of the wrong discipline could prove disastrous.

TRIBUNAL OF MORE THAN ONE ARBITRATOR

It must be pretty lonely work sitting as an arbitrator, Thomasina said. One of my friends' father is in the maritime field and he is an arbitrator, but I seem to recall him saying that he sits with two other arbitrators. How does that work? Well, you're quite right, I said, not all tribunals are sole arbitrators. In the maritime and commodity fields there are usually three arbitrators, often two arbitrators and an umpire, who usually steps in if the arbitrators, who are appointed by each party, disagree; he then takes over and operates as the sole arbitrator.

In other disciplines, where the arbitration agreement calls for two arbitrators—again usually appointed by each party—the Act provides for them to appoint a chairman. In this case, or where the tribunal comprises three arbitrators, the majority decision prevails.

It can be beneficial to have more than one arbitrator where the dispute comprises a mixture of technical and legal issues—with technical and legal arbitrators being chosen—but, of course, I said, it is much more expensive than just having a sole arbitrator. In addition, the process is usually much slower on the bigger international cases due to the difficulty of finding slots in all three arbitrators' diaries.

So, I said, if you're happy with all that, let us move on. Thomasina readily agreed. She was warming to the subject and wanted to know more.

ADVANTAGES OF ARBITRATION

Before we went any further and looked at the preliminary meeting, I suggested to Thomasina that we should summarise where we have got to and consider the advantages of arbitration over the other alternative forms of dispute resolution.

First of all there is the ability of the parties to choose their own tribunal. This, of course, is not an option available to them if their dispute is tried in a court of law.

Next, there is the question of confidentiality or privacy. This can be immensely important, I told her, where there are commercially sensitive issues. For example, I have no doubt that many of Thomasina's clients would not wish their disputes to be common knowledge, particularly where their dispute concerns a secret process, the details of which they would wish to guard from competitors. Court proceedings are not private and such confidentiality therefore could not be guaranteed.

Then there is a question of speed. Court lists tend to be long and it can take many months, or even years in some instances, for a case to be heard. That is not so in arbitration. In choosing their tribunal the parties can ensure that their appointed arbitrator is in a position to hear the case expeditiously. Not only will the case get heard much earlier in arbitration but, because of the arbitrator's ability to tailor the procedure to the dispute, a speedier resolution can be assured.

Cost is another factor. Certainly arbitration *should* be cheaper than litigation. Indeed, I said, many innovations practised by arbitrators are finding their way into court proceedings—for example, the limitations on orality; limitation on discovery; witnesses' statements taken as evidence-in-chief *et al*. What does that mean? asked Thomasina. It means, I told her, that having written his or her proof of evidence, that statement stands as that witness's proof of evidence and instead of taking the witness through it line by line, as has happened in the past and indeed still happens in some courts

18 What is arbitration?

(although admittedly now to a lesser extent), this witness goes straight into cross-examination.

Above all, it is flexibility of procedure which should give arbitration a substantial advantage over litigation, I explained. We will see when we come to go through the agenda for the preliminary meeting.

Another advantage that arbitration enjoys over litigation is that the parties can choose their own form of representation, which they cannot necessarily do if the case is heard in court where there are restrictions on who can appear on their behalf. No such restriction exists before the arbitrator. This is a particular advantage where lay parties are involved who do not wish, or cannot afford, to instruct lawyers, perhaps because of the small amount of money at stake.

[margin note: don't need to be a lawyer to represent someone at an arbitration]

Something we will touch on when we get to the end of this process is the question of appeals against the arbitrator's award, I told Thomasina. All you need to know at this stage is that there is very limited scope for appealing such award. A greater degree of finality is imported into the dispute than you would get if the case were heard in court.

Finally, I emphasised once more that arbitrators are not bound by the rules of court, although there are some instances where it is prudent for them to follow a similar line if they are to be seen to be acting judicially. Hopefully, I told her, this will become clearer as we go through and examine the process.

Although the arbitrator is generally fairly free to run the arbitration in the manner in which he sees fit, the courts have a role to play in support of the processes which we will look at in more detail later. But suffice it to say, at this stage, that the courts provide a safeguard against an arbitrator's unreasonable behaviour, both in terms of procedure and his fees, as well as providing a mechanism for deciding jurisdictional points, preliminary points of law and for appeals against his award on a very limited grounds.

I asked Thomasina if all was clear so far. She said, she thought so—but did not sound very convincing—but, no doubt, she said, all would become clear as we went through.

How does the process begin, following the arbitrator's appointment, she asked? Presumably he gives them some indication of how he intends to proceed? I suggested that the best way that I could answer this was to go through an example of a typical letter, which I send on these occasions (see opposite).

OK, you have been appointed. Now what? What is the next step?

CHAPTER 4

THE ARBITRATOR'S OPENING SHOT

The letter I chose to illustrate the arbitrator's opening shot to the parties was one written for a dispute between a builder and the owner of a Georgian manor house, who entered into a contract for its conversion into a nursing home for the elderly infirm and it all went wrong. We referred to this dispute in the office as *The Sanctuary House Case*, as this was the name that the owner of the house, Mr Bliss, gave to the Home once the conversion was complete.

The parties had entered into a JCT form of contract and, accordingly, the dispute was governed by the JCT Arbitration Rules. Why so? asked Thomasina. Because, I said, all JCT standard forms incorporate a provision to the effect that any disputes referred to arbitration under that contract will be governed by such rules. Thus, in writing to the parties it is essential to make this point.

I suggested that we looked at the letter paragraph by paragraph:

LETTER FOLLOWING APPOINTMENT

D. MARK CATO MSc FRICS FCIArb
REGISTERED ARBITRATOR & MEDIATOR
Construction Dispute Resolution—Arbitration and Mediation

Lantern Thatch
Clavering Essex CB11 4QT
Telephone: 01799 550 844
Facsimilie: 01799 550 302

your ref

our ref DMC/4800.4   23 October 1998

Reliable Builders Ltd   Sanctuary House Ltd
Snape Yard   Registered Office
Woodbridge   Matthews House
Suffolk   Main Street
                               Suffolk
FAO Harry Hocking
                               FAO William Bliss

FAX & POST

Gentlemen

In the matter of an arbitration between Reliable Builders Ltd v Sanctuary House Ltd in connection with works at Sanctuary House, Woodbridge, Suffolk

1. I have been appointed by the President of the Royal Institution of Chartered Surveyors (RICS) as Arbitrator in the above Arbitration, pursuant to an application to the RICS and my appointment dated 22 October 1998, received under cover of their letter 22 October 1998. The RICS specifically request me to send copies of the Case Details to each party. These are attached hereto.

2. I confirm that the arbitration is to be conducted in accord-

Letter following appointment

ance with the JCT 1998 Edition of the Construction Industry Model Arbitration Rules (JCT Arbitration Rules).

3. I confirm that the notification date for the purpose of the Rule 6.3.1 is the date of this letter, namely 23 October 1998.

4. As the parties will appreciate, under these Rules, the notification date is the date on which I inform them of my appointment, after which the Preliminary Meeting (if any) has to be held within 21 days (Rule 6.3.1); from thence the entire timetable is geared to this date.

5. The parties are no doubt aware that a new Arbitration Act came into force on 31 January 1997 and this Act governs this reference.

6. Under Rule 6.2, the parties are to provide me with the following (copied to the other side)
   (a) a note stating the nature of the dispute with an estimate of the amounts in issue;
   (b) a view as to the need for and length of any hearing;
   (c) proposals as to the form of procedure appropriate to the dispute.
As I am bound to proceed without unnecessary delay, I request the parties to provide this information no later than 5.00 p.m. 30 October 1998.

7. If, then, from the brief information I have available concerning this dispute, it seems to me that a Preliminary Meeting is warranted and I therefore propose holding such a meeting with the parties on one of the following dates and times **in my order of preference.**

10.30 a.m. on 10, 11, 12 or 13 November 1998.

These dates and times are offered on the assumption that this meeting will be held at The Fleet Arbitration Centre, 6th Floor, Hulton House, 161–166 Fleet Street, London EC4A 2DY (telephone number 0171 936 3111) unless the parties agree to hold it at one of their offices or at the offices of one of their representatives, in which case I may need to reconsider both times and dates offered—please liaise over this and inform me of your joint decision. I will leave it to the Claimant to make the necessary arrangements. I am holding all these days and times so please let me know, as soon as possible, but in any event within seven days, where this meeting is to be held. If you wish to contact me via my fax number in order to confirm this, by all means do so.

22 The arbitrator's opening shot

In making a decision concerning the necessity for a Preliminary Meeting, I will of course take into account any agreement of the parties.

8. If I should decide that a Preliminary Meeting is necessary or desirable, then as soon as I receive confirmation of the venue date and time for this Preliminary Meeting I will issue an Order for Directions and an Agenda. May I say this however concerning the Agenda. It is a comprehensive list of all the matters which I believe I need to consider with the parties at the inception of any dispute governed by this relatively new Arbitration Act.

It will be seen that the Agenda covers various options from "Documents Only" through to a full procedure involving a Hearing. Thus, much of the Agenda *may* not apply to this reference. Please therefore consider it as an aide memoire from which we may pick and choose those elements which will assist us, or to tailor a procedure which will ensure a cost-effective and speedy solution to this dispute.

9. As pointed out earlier this dispute is governed by the JCT Arbitration Rules as well as the overriding provisions of the Arbitration Act 1996 (AA '96).

The mandatory provisions of this Act apply in any event, but, where the JCT Rules cover any non-mandatory provisions of the Act then the Rules can be taken as being an express agreement of the parties under the Act.

10. In general then—and bearing in mind the comments above—at the Preliminary Meeting I shall expect the parties, or their representatives, as appropriate, to address me either on their joint decision as to which of Rules 7, 8 & 9 is to apply to the conduct of the arbitration or, if no joint agreement is reached, then to let me have their views on the appropriate Rule. In this regard bear in mind Rule 6.3.2. In order to do this it is imperative that the parties or their representatives be fully conversant with the nature of the dispute or difference and that areas of agreement and disagreement are fully canvassed and identified to me. The parties should consider liaising before the Preliminary Meeting with a view to narrowing issues as far as possible. I shall also be asking the parties to assist me in estimating the likely length of any hearing, in the light of information sent to me previously and in the event that Rule 9 applies to the conduct of the arbitration, as a preliminary to any exercise of my power to limit the parties' recoverable costs (s.65 AA '96).

11. Please inform me, and the other party, of the names and status of those who are expected to attend the Preliminary

Meeting, and I should like to have this information not later than seven days prior to the meeting date. Please note that I do like to see a senior representative from each party at this meeting, not merely the parties' representatives.

12. I remind the parties that the JCT Arbitration Rules contain certain very strict timetables in connection with the delivery of statements. Failure to serve any statement in accordance with the prescribed or directed timetable under these Rules can involve the parties in very serious consequences.

13. As required by Rule 14.2, would each party please notify the other and me of the address for service upon them of statements, documents and notices referred to in the Rules, including facsimile, telex or e-mail numbers where appropriate.

14. You will find enclosed a copy of my Terms and Conditions* and I would appreciate it if each of you would sign your copy and return it to me forthwith, together with the deposit cheque, as specified, from the Claimant.

15. Should either party not be familiar with the JCT Arbitration Rules, copies can be obtained from The RICS Bookshop, The Royal Institution of Chartered Surveyors, 12 Great George St, SW1P 3AD. I am also happy to recommend an excellent book on the Arbitration Act: *The Arbitration Act 1996—A Commentary* by Harris, Planterose and Tecks, Blackwell Science, available from the Chartered Institute of Arbitrators, telephone 0171 837 4483.

Yours faithfully

**D Mark Cato MSc FRICS FCIArb
Arbitrator**

*With hard copy only.

24 The arbitrator's opening shot

I suggested to Thomasina that she could learn quite a lot if we examined and discussed this letter clause by clause:

1. Confirms by whom the arbitrator has been appointed and gives the date of his appointment.

Whether the appointment has been made by the parties in agreement or by a third party appointing body, it is as well to record this to pre-empt either party dissenting from it at a later stage.

2. This confirms that the arbitration is being conducted under Rules—in this case the JCT Arbitration Rules.

This is a construction case and, therefore, it is governed the JCT Rules as the dispute arises out of one of the JCT family of contracts. There are many other institutional Rules, not only for construction disputes such as the ICE Procedure but many scheme arbitrations, all of which have their own Rules; which, I told Thomasina, we would consider later.

3. The notification date for the purpose of these Rules is then given.

This is important in terms of time limits that may be imposed upon the parties by statute or, indeed, by the arbitration agreement itself, for commencing an action under that particular contract.

4. This merely reminds the parties that a Preliminary Meeting (if there is one) has to be held within 21 days of the arbitrator's appointment and is specific to the JCT Arbitration Rules.

5. This clause reminds the parties about the new Arbitration Act which governs the this reference.

This clause will fall away shortly as all references begun after 31 January 1997 are governed by the new Act. However, for a period it was necessary to mention the new arbitration Act to cover the transitional period between the previous Arbitration Acts 1950 and 1979 and the new 1996 Act.

6. This requires the parties to brief the arbitrator on the nature of the dispute and how best it should be resolved.

I believe that this was included more in hope than expectation. I shall consider myself very fortunate to have such full information so early on and in advance of a preliminary meeting, unless, of course, the parties decided that they did not require such a meeting.

7. Informs the parties that, from the information sent to the arbitrator it appears to him that a preliminary meeting is appropriate.

I stressed the importance of this clause to Thomasina. No arbitrator should assume that a preliminary meeting is essential in every instance. Many small disputes would not warrant the expense of a preliminary meeting, where the arbitrator's costs alone could amount to, say, £500. When an arbitrator is appointed he is usually sent very limited information on the nature of the dispute, although Rule 6.2 has attempted to address that by asking the parties to inform the arbitrator of the nature of the dispute; an estimate of the amounts in dispute; whether they consider that a hearing is necessary and if so how long it need to be; and finally their proposals on the form of procedure to be followed. It is on this information that he has to decide whether it is necessary to hold a preliminary meeting or whether he can deal with the whole reference by "documents only". I told Thomasina that I would devote a few minutes to talking about "documents only" arbitrations a little later on in our discussion.

What would you do, she said, if you decide that the dispute is appropriate for "documents only" and one of the parties responds by requesting a meeting? In that case, I said, depending on the information available to me, I should probably reply that I did not consider it necessary, but if that party insisted I would certainly be prepared to hold such a meeting. But in the event that I subsequently found that such a meeting was not necessary, I would have to bear this in mind in deciding who bore the costs of this meeting.

I asked Thomasina to note that I identified where the meeting should be held and the dates offered to the parties for this meeting. I also planted the suggestion in the minds of the parties that, in order to save costs, this meeting could be held at the offices of one of the parties or their representatives, but it was up to them to liaise and make this decision. In the event of lack of agreement between the parties I made it clear to them where I intended to hold the meeting. She should also note that I made it clear to the parties that if they wish to contact me they could do so via my fax number, not, by implication, by telephone direct.

8. This is the early warning about the comprehensive agenda that I intend to send to the parties, which relates to the various options open to me, and indeed to them, under the new Arbitration Act.

9. Confirms that the dispute is covered by the JCT Arbitration Rules.

This is the first opportunity the parties have to inform the arbitrator that they consider that the JCT Rules do not apply.

I also remind the parties that the mandatory provisions of the Arbitration Act 1996 apply, in the event, and any part of the JCT Rules which covers non-mandatory provisions of the Act will be taken as an express agreement of the parties under the Act. The importance of such express agreement will become clearer to her, I told Thomasina, as we go through the agenda.

10. Here I spell out what it is I expect of the parties or the representatives at the preliminary meeting. I remind them that there is a choice between various options under the JCT Rules and that if they cannot agree then they should let me have their views on which of the rules they consider most appropriate.

As Thomasina was not familiar with the JCT Rules, I pointed out that Rule 8 was the "documents only" procedure. Rule 9 was the one that provides for a full hearing and Rule 7 is a short procedure suitable for minor disputes—for example, where the issue is one merely of quality.

The second paragraph of item 9 gives the parties the first warning shot about my intention to impose, or at least to consider

[Handwritten note at top: Arbitrator has power to limit winner's recoverable costs]

imposing, a limitation on the winning party's recoverable costs. This is a power that I now enjoy under AA '96, provided, that is, that the parties do not agree otherwise. This is a real weapon in the arbitrator's armoury for ensuring that one of the two major objectives of making arbitration more cost-effective than litigation is maintained.

11. This paragraph not only requires the parties to inform me of names of those who intend to appear at the preliminary meeting but urges the parties to send a senior representative from the principals involved.

In other words, it asks them to send a decision-maker from each side. As this may be the only time that the arbitrator will meet these principals until the case gets to a hearing, perhaps six or nine months later, one objective of seeking their presence is that when they leave this preliminary meeting they do so in the full knowledge that their dispute is in good, safe and impartial hands.

The other reason for having these party representatives at the preliminary meeting is that it may be the first time that a senior decision-taker from each side has really got to grips with what the dispute is all about. This can often lead to an early settlement, effecting a saving of money and senior management time. Thus in such an event the arbitrator would have done a good job.

[Handwritten margin notes: early settlement]

12. Here I remind the parties of the strict timetables imposed by these Rules and of the serious consequences if they fail to meet the dates for the service of their statements, as directed by me.

If parties are representing themselves then the consequences of any failure to comply with my directions must be brought to their attention. See paragraph 15 below.

13. This is simply a requirement of the Rules, for each party to inform the other where it wishes documents to be served.

It may be, for example, that the only address that one party has for the other is its registered office, which could, of course, be overseas.

Claimant to pay arbitrator's costs until winner is determined

28 The arbitrator's opening shot

14. Here is the first mention of my Terms and Conditions and my request for them to sign and return them to me.

I also pointed out to Thomasina that she would note that I was requesting a deposit cheque from the claimant. I have always taken the view that all of my fees and expenses should be paid by the claimant—i.e. the person who has mounted the case—in the first place, until such time as I decide who is the loser, and therefore the party who should then pay the winning party's cost and my fees and expenses.

I believe it to be a mistake to do as some arbitrators do, and seek payment of their fees in equal tranches from both parties. What happens, I said, if one pays and the other doesn't? Where does that leave the arbitrator?

15. Finally, some helpful advice—more for the lay party than the lawyer—as to where they can obtain copies of the Rules and a relatively inexpensive book which will assist them with this reference.

Sometimes parties represent themselves and do not engage solicitors to assist them. In these cases, where institutional Rules are involved, the parties really need to obtain a copy of those Rules and familiarise themselves with their provisions.

If there is any aspect of those Rules which a party does not understand then the arbitrator can, of course, explain his understanding to them in the presence of the other party, giving that other party the opportunity of adding to or qualifying what the arbitrator has said. It is for this reason that I am only too pleased to direct them to the RICS bookshop and to recommend the book set out in this paragraph.

Well, I said, that concludes our examination of the first letter that I send to the parties. Had Thomasina any questions? I asked. No, she said, that was all pretty clear. I suggested to her that we had done quite enough for our first session and that we should call it a day. Next time we met we would start on the preliminary meeting, which I have always considered to be one of the most important steps, if not *the* most important step, in the whole process. After all, I said, it sets the tone for the entire reference.

Thomasina then asked if she could invite Charley, her boyfriend, to our next meeting. She reminded me that he was a rent review arbitrator's pupil and it would be interesting to hear what he had to say about the way he and his pupil master conduct their preliminary meeting. I agreed that that would be a splendid idea and encouraged her to invite him.

Thomasina then departed and I was able to get back to some real work!

CHAPTER 5

THE PRELIMINARY MEETING

Having whetted Thomasina's appetite by discussing arbitration at our first session, I received a telephone call from her, a few days later, asking if she could come round and continue our discussion, and bring Charley with her, as I had agreed. As it happened, a large case for which I had been asked to set aside several weeks had just settled, and thus I had time on my hands. I suggested that she should come round two days later and spend the day with me, so that we could really get to grips with the next stage of the arbitral process—the preliminary meeting. In the meantime, I said that I would send her a copy of my standard agenda so that she could study this before we met.

Two days later, the young arrived. Virtually the first comment Thomasina made concerned the length of the agenda—17 pages of it in all. Was it really necessary to go into so much detail at such an early stage? she asked. I said that I had to be quite honest about it, this agenda was very much my own device; many other, highly respectable, arbitrators took a different line from me. Some of them, indeed, had only a single page agenda with bullet points for discussion. (Charley then produced his two-page agenda, which reinforced my point. I suggested that, rather than confuse the poor girl by comparing the two agendas, we should go through his when we had completed reviewing mine. That being so, I asked him to forgive me if I tended to direct my remarks to Thomasina at this stage of the discussion. He quite understood, he said. I must say, I was quite impressed—he seems a nice boy.)

Reverting to my agenda then, as I said to them, I take the "full monty" approach. When I revised this agenda following the enactment of AA '96, I decided that I would set out as much as possible in advance of the preliminary meeting, so that the parties could come to that meeting having given mature consideration to the points which I intended to raise. It is all a matter of individual choice, I told her. That is the beauty of arbitration, which I cannot stress too strongly—flexibility of approach. What works for you is probably the best procedure.

Having got that lecture off my chest we then turned to the agenda itself.

THE AGENDA

IN THE MATTER OF THE ARBITRATION ACT 1996

AND

IN THE MATTER OF AN ARBITRATION UNDER THE JCT 1998 EDITION OF THE CONSTRUCTION INDUSTRY MODEL ARBITRATION RULES (CIMAR)

BETWEEN

THE RELIABLE BUILDING CO. LTD.   **Claimant**

and

SANCTUARY HOUSE LTD.   **Respondent**

PRELIMINARY MEETING

To be held at the Fleet Arbitration Centre, 161 Fleet St., London, EC4 at 10.30 a.m. on 11 November 1998

AGENDA

(Note: Bracketed references thus (s.xxx) are to the relevant sections of the Arbitration Act 1996 and in all cases these sections of the Act are to be read in conjunction with the relevant section of the Rules.)

1.00 Introductions.

Confirmation of identity and status of Parties.

2.00 Appointment (s.16(1))

2.01 A copy of Notice of Arbitration required to be produced for the Arbitrator.

2.02 Confirmation that the Arbitrator has been validly appointed.

2.03 Original contract—required to be produced for Arbitrator's inspection.

3.00 Jurisdiction

3.01 Note: under Rule 4.1 the Arbitrator may rule on his own substantive jurisdiction (s.30).

3.02 If this should prove necessary, the arbitrator may either:

3.02.1 Rule on it in an award on jurisdiction (s.31(4)(a)), or

3.02.2 Deal with the objection in his award on the merits (s.31(4)(b)).

4.00 Seat and Applicable Law

Confirmation that the seat of the arbitration shall be England (s.3) and that the applicable law shall be the law of England and Wales (s.46).

5.00 Commencement of the Arbitration

Confirmation of the date for the commencement of the arbitration (s.14) notification date—Rule 6.3.1.

6.00 Identify Items in Dispute

6.01 Outline of Claimant's case.

6.02 Outline of Respondent's case.

6.03 Discussion of issues—relative importance. Are some not worth pursuing? Keep this under constant review.

Identify and record principal areas of agreement and disagreement.

6.04 An agreed list of issues which remain to be determined to be handed to the Arbitrator not later than the close of the hearing.

7.00 Arbitrator's General Powers

7.01 It shall be for the Arbitrator to decide all procedural matters, subject to the right of the parties to agree any matter, and this includes the power to direct:

7.01.1 When and where any part of the proceedings is to be held (s.34(2)(a))

7.01.2 The language to be used in the proceedings and where translations are to be supplied (s.34(2)(b))

7.01.3 The use of written statements and the extent to which they can be amended (s.34(2)(c))

7.01.4 Which documents, or classes of documents, should be disclosed between and produced by the parties and at what stage (s.34(2)(d))

7.01.5 The extent to which he shall take the initiative in ascertaining the facts and the law (s.34(2)(g))

7.01.6 Whether and to what extent there should be oral and written evidence or submissions (s.34(2)(h)) and, if there are to be oral proceedings, how witnesses are to be examined (s.38(5))

7.01.7 On the award of interest (s.49(2)–(5)).

7.02 The Arbitrator shall have

7.02.1 The general powers exercised by the Tribunal (s.38(4)–(6))

7.02.2 Power to make a declaratory award (s.48(3))

7.02.3 Powers, as set out in s.41(3)–(7), in case of party's default

7.02.4 Authority to record any agreement reached at the Preliminary Meeting on behalf of the parties (s.5).

7.03 The Arbitrator shall have power to:

7.03.1 Appoint experts (including a tribunal appointed expert, if agreed—see 10.03.6.7 below—take legal advice or appoint an assessor (s.37)

7.03.2 Order a party to do or refrain from doing anything (s.48(5)(a))

7.03.3 Order specific performance of a contract (other than a contract relating to land) (s.48(5)(b))

7.03.4 Order the rectification, setting aside or cancellation of a deed or other document (s.48(5)(c))

36 The preliminary meeting

   7.03.5 Make a provisional award (s.39). Note: the arbitrator may exercise the powers under Rule 10—Provisional Relief—after application by a party or of his own motion after giving due notice to the parties

   7.03.6 Fix the time within which any order or direction is to be complied with and may extend or reduce the time at any stage (s.34(3)).

  7.04 An application to the court for an order requiring a party to comply with a peremptory order may be made only by or with the permission of the arbitrator (s.42(20)).

8.00 Joinder/Consolidation (s.35)

  8.01 Is there any possibility of joinder of parties?

  8.02 Is there any agreement on consolidation with any other arbitral proceedings or, alternatively, concurrent hearings?

9.00 Issues

  9.01 Can either party identify one or more issues which, if decided as a preliminary issue, could dispense with all, or a substantial element of, the dispute?

  9.02 The arbitrator may:

   9.02.1 Decide what are the issues to be determined

   9.02.2 Decide whether or not to give an award on part of the claims submitted (s.47).

10.00 Proceedings

JCT 1998 Edition of the Construction Industry Model Arbitration Rules applies (s.4(3))
(Note: Under these Rules the parties may not, without the agreement of the arbitrator, amend the rules, or impose procedures in conflict with them)
Most cost effective procedure?
  Documents only or attended Hearing? (s.34(2)(h))
  Statement of Case/Formal/Informal Pleadings? (s.34(2)(c))
   In general terms if Statement of Case, such Statement

shall set out the factual and legal basis relied upon. (See individual Rules for specific requirements)
(Note: Arbitrator's duty to adopt procedures suitable to the circumstances and to avoid unnecessary delay or expense (s.33).
Parties shall do all things necessary for the proper and expeditious conduct of the proceedings (s.40))

10.01 If Rule 8—Documents Only is to apply

Unsuitable where a serious dispute over relevant facts.
Issues need to be framed with more precision than when attended Hearing.

10.01.1 Timetable (See Rule 8.2)

Date for Claimant's written Statement, evidence, witness proofs and experts' reports (if any).
Period for Respondent's written Statement, evidence, witness proofs and experts' reports (if any).
Period for Claimant's written response.
Period for Respondent's written Reply.

10.01.2 Classification

If after reading the parties' written statements, the arbitrator decides that he requires further clarification of any part of those statements, by an interview with the parties or otherwise, or requires some further documentation which he considers is essential for him properly to decide on the matters in dispute, then he may require such clarification or further document by notice in writing to the Claimant or the Respondent as appropriate and shall serve a copy of that notice upon the party not required to provide such clarification or further document.

Such clarification by an interview with the parties or otherwise shall be obtained in accordance with the directions of the Arbitrator and such further document shall be supplied to the Arbitrator with a copy to the other party by the Claimant or Respondent forthwith upon receipt of the notice in writing from the Arbitrator (s.34(2)(g)).

10.01.3 Power to order Hearing

After reading the parties' written statements the arbitrator

38 The preliminary meeting

may direct that there will be a hearing of not more than one day at which he will put questions to the parties and/or to any witness. In this event the parties will also have a reasonable opportunity to comment on any additional information given to the arbitrator. *(in writing or at a further hearing?)*

10.02 If Rule 7—Short Procedure with Hearing is to apply

Only suitable for "quality" disputes requiring some summary decision.

Each party shall bear its own costs [s.60] and half the costs of the arbitrator's fees and expenses, unless otherwise directed (Rule 13.4.1).

Each party must deliver their written Statement of Case 7 days *before* the Hearing. The Hearing to take place within 21 days of this Rule becoming applicable.

10.03 If Rule 9—Full procedure with Hearing is to apply

Need not *all* be oral (s.34(2)(h)). Note Rule 6.3.
For disputes which require examination/cross-examination of witnesses of fact.

10.03.1 Consider whether Scott Schedule desirable.

10.03.2 Timetable

The following timetable shall be followed, unless otherwise directed, viz:

10.03.2.1 The Claimant shall, within 28 days after the date when Rule 9 becomes applicable, serve a *Statement of Claim*. *(Claim or Case?)*

10.03.2.2 If the Claimant serves a Statement of Case within the 28 days directed the Respondent *shall*, within 28 days after service of the Claimant's Statement of Claim, serve a *Statement of Defence* to the Claimant's Statement of Claim and a Statement of any *Counterclaim*.

10.03.2.3 If the Respondent serves a Statement of Defence within the 28 days directed the Claimant *may*, within 28 days after such service, serve a Statement of *Reply to the Defence*.

10.03.2.4 If the Respondent serves a Statement of Counterclaim within the 28 days directed the Claimant *shall*, within 28 days after such service, serve a Statement of Defence to the Respondent's Counterclaim.

10.03.2.5 If the Claimant serves a Statement of Defence to the Respondent's Statement of Counterclaim within the 28 days directed the Respondent *may*, within 14 days after such service, serve a Statement of Reply to the Defence.

10.03.2.6 The parties' exchanged Statements and Replies shall accord with the following guidelines:
(a) each Statement should contain the facts and matters of opinion which are intended to be established by evidence and may include a Statement of any relevant point of law which will be contended for;
(b) a Statement should contain sufficient particulars to enable the other party to answer each allegation without recourse to general denials;
(c) a Statement may include or refer to evidence to be adduced if this will assist in defining the issues to be determined;
(d) the reliefs or remedies sought, for instance specific monetary losses, must be stated in such a way that they can be answered or admitted;
(e) all Statements should adopt a common system of numbering or identification of sections to facilitate analysis of issues. Particulars given in schedule form should anticipate the need to incorporate replies.

10.03.2.7 No provision for Further and Better Particulars (But note Rules 9.3 & 9.4)

Consider each party serving a Notice to Admit and/or Interrogatories or arbitrator putting written questions to parties, with questions and written answers copied to the other side (s.34(2)(e)).

If Further and Better Particulars prove necessary, at the discretion of Arbitrator,

Requests are to be made within 7 days of the delivery of the Statement ("Pleading") to which they refer.

Note: The criteria adopted to determine whether Further and Better Particulars are reasonable are:

1. Is it capable of answer?
2. Will it assist the questioning party to understand the case against it or to investigate it?
3. Is it on the critical path and/or does it form the logic necessary to reach the Award?

Consent is likely to be refused where—

1. Questions are oppressive and it appears that the intention is to distract the answering party from other matters.
2. They fail to go to an issue on the critical path.

Replies to Requests for Further and Better Particulars are to be made within 7 days of the Request.

Note: The period for delivery of any subsequent Statement ("Pleading") shall be extended by the time which elapses between the delivery of a Request for Further and Better Particulars and the deliver of the answer thereto.

Pleadings (service of Statements) shall be deemed to be closed 7 days after the delivery of the last of the above-mentioned Statement ("Pleading") or 7 days after the expiry of the period allowed for delivery of any Statement ("Pleading") if no further Statement ("Pleading") has been delivered.

10.03.3 Witness Statements

10.03.3.1 Consider whether any proofs of evidence/rebuttals, whether of fact or expert opinion, be appended to Statements.

10.03.3.2 Alternatively, if not appended to Statements, Witnesses' proofs of evidence, if agreed, to be exchanged simultaneously and copied to the Arbitrator. Exchanged proofs to be admitted as evidence in chief.
Rebuttals?
Date of exchange? (Normally 4 weeks after close of Pleadings).

[handwritten: for a witness to be called at a hearing, there must first be a written proof of evidence.]

The agenda

10.03.3.3 Except by my leave (which will only be given in special circumstances), no witness may be called at the Hearing unless a written proof of evidence has been provided in accordance with the preceding paragraph.

10.03.3.4 No further evidence in chief may be adduced by a witness on any matter which has not been included in that witness's proof of evidence either specifically or by reference to a document or documents listed or produced in accordance with 10.03.2.6 above.

All Statements together with their supporting documents, served under these Rules shall, once proved, be admitted as documentary evidence.

10.03.4 Experts

[handwritten: ? and have one agreed Expert]

10.03.4.1 If Experts engaged, parties to attempt to agree joint instructions. Such agreement/non-agreement to be notified to the Arbitrator.

10.03.4.2 Date for exchange of their reports/rebuttals.

10.03.4.3 Inspection access for experts—if necessary?

10.03.4.4 Experts will meet, "open"/"without prejudice" to endeavour to narrow the issues. What authority do they have? Privilege shall be waived for any matter agreed at these meetings.

10.03.4.5 The Experts to meet not later than 28 days after the close of "Pleadings".

They shall endeavour to narrow the issues and to agree facts as facts, figures as figures etc. as far as possible.

The Experts shall prepare, date and sign a note of the facts and opinions upon which they are agreed, and of the issues upon which they cannot agree. A copy of such note to be exchanged and delivered to the Arbitrator within 14 days of their meeting but in any event no later than 56 days before the Hearing.

10.03.4.6 Not later than 42 days before the hearing, each party may address written questions to the opposing expert on the content of that expert's report to which that expert will be required to give written responses not later than 7 days after receipt of those questions.

Not later than 7 days after receipt of these written responses the party who posed the question may serve a further written comment.

All of the above to be copied to the Arbitrator, who may, not later than 21 days before the hearing, send written questions to the parties to which their experts should respond. These Replies to be sent to the Arbitrator not later than 7 days thereafter and rebuttals or comments on these responses may be sent to the Arbitrator, copied to the other side, not later than 7 days before the hearing.

The intention is either to avoid, if possible, oral examination of experts, or restrict it to the major issues in difference between them. Whether any oral examination of experts is allowed will, in any event, provided the parties do not agree otherwise, be at the discretion of the Arbitrator.

Alternatively:

10.03.4.7 Consider a tribunal appointed expert for appropriate issues.

In which case the parties are:

1 To agree who the tribunal's expert should be, in consultation with the Arbitrator.

2 To agree on the wording of the issue(s) to be submitted to the tribunal's expert and in the absence of agreement the Arbitrator will decide on this wording.

3 To define the scope of the tribunal's expert's enquiries and, in the absence of agreement, this matter is to be decided by the Arbitrator taking into account the parties' submissions.

Not later than 28 days of the close of Pleadings the tribunal appointed expert is to deliver a Draft Report to each party.

Within 14 days of the delivery of this

Report a representative of the parties is to meet with the tribunal's expert to discuss his Draft Report. The discretion whether to amend this Draft Report, following submissions from the parties' representatives, to be entirely that of tribunal's expert.

Not later than 14 days after the meeting between the tribunal's expert and the parties' representatives the tribunal's expert shall deliver a copy of his Final Report to the tribunal, copied to the parties.

Should either party wish to cross-examine the tribunal's expert on any matter contained in his Final Report (on any issue within the tribunal's expert's term of reference, whether or not covered by his Final Report) then, not later than 7 days before the hearing, notice must be given in writing of the matters on which the cross-examination is desired, to be delivered to the tribunal's expert, copied to the Arbitrator and the other side.

At the hearing any cross examination of the tribunal's expert may be conducted by a party appointed expert rather than the party's general advocate, if that is the party's preference.

10.03.5 Disclosure of Documents

    10.03.5.1 There will be no provision for disclosure (discovery) of documents. Documents on which parties wish to rely must be disclosed and included with their Statements.

    10.03.5.2 However, if one party can satisfy the Arbitrator that the other party is likely to have in his possession, or power, documents which might be helpful to that party's case or damaging to that other party's case which are not included with the supporting documentation of that party's case then the

Arbitrator, provided he is satisfied of the relevance of the documents, will initially invite voluntary disclosure, in default of which he will order selective disclosure—Rules 5.2 & 9.4 (s.34(2)(d)).

10.03.5.3 In addition to those documents disclosed and included with the parties' Statements, each party shall append to its initial Statement a list of all other documents in its possession or power, under main category headings, which may be relevant to the issues in dispute.

10.03.6 General

10.03.6.1 *Service of Statements/Documents*

In relation to service of Statements by facsimile, if documentation is voluminous consider agreeing that such documents should be sent separately by first class post or courier at the same time as the facsimile Statement and that this shall be regarded as good service.

Copies of Statements to be sent to the Arbitrator at the same time as to the other party.

If either party fails to comply with timetable the other party to notify Arbitrator immediately of non-service and/or late service.

10.03.6.2 *Communication*

All communications to the Arbitrator to be copied to the other side, and to be in writing—not telephone—but may be made by fax, in which case a further copy must be sent forthwith by first class post or delivered by hand.

10.03.6.3 *Extensions of Time* (See Rule 5.6)

All applications for extension of time

extension of time request? Must be made before time period ends

The agenda

must be made to the Arbitrator, in writing, before time expires—copy to other party.

10.03.6.4 *Offers* (See Rule 13.9)

Sealed offers—*modus operandi*?

10.03.7 Pre-Hearing Review

10.03.7.1 To consider all outstanding issues which need to be narrowed and clarified. Are some issues not worth pursuing?

narrowing issues

10.03.7.2 Arbitrator to decide which witnesses he requires to hear on what issues.

which witnesses

10.03.7.3 Rule 9.4.1 provides that not later than 14 days after the receipt of the last of the Statements and documents referred to in Rule 9.2, the Arbitrator will notify the parties of the date of the Oral Hearing and other matters listed in Rule 9.4. This is generally too late—these matters should either be dealt with at the Preliminary Meeting or by application of the parties or direction of the Arbitrator during the interlocutory period.

10.03.8 Hearing

10.03.8.1 *Sitting*
Each sitting day will be from 10.00 a.m. to 5.00 p.m. with one hour's recess for luncheon.

10.03.8.2 *Estimated Duration*
Provisional Date? Total length in days? 4 day sitting week.

10.03.8.3 *Venue/Accommodation*
Claimant will arrange suitable accommodation in consultation with the Respondent and the Arbitrator. In the

claimant resp to book venue

absence of agreement between the parties the Claimant shall book accommodation at a venue to be directed by the Arbitrator (s.34(2)(a)).

10.03.8.4 *Hearing bundle*
Parties to deliver, to the Arbitrator, not less than 7 days before the Hearing, a Hearing bundle of documents properly paginated, properly and fully indexed with relevant passages of text upon which reliance will be placed suitably highlighted.

After delivery of this bundle the Arbitrator will wait 24 hours before reading it in order to give the parties the opportunity to check if, inadvertently, any "without prejudice" material has found its way into the bundle. In which case, on being informed of this, the Arbitrator's secretary will locate the document and return it, unread by the Arbitrator, to the parties.

A core bundle of principal documents?

What do the parties want the Arbitrator to read prior to the Hearing?

Nothing in the bundle is to be taken as read by the Arbitrator until adduced at the Hearing.

10.03.8.5 *Rules of Evidence*
The Arbitrator is not bound by the strict rules of evidence and shall determine the admissibility, relevance and weight of any material sought to be tendered on any matters of fact or opinion by any party (s.34(2)(f)).

10.03.8.6 *Evidence on Oath*
All evidence shall be on oath or affirmation (s.38).

10.03.8.7 *Limitation on Orality*

> Time allowed for examination-in-chief and cross examination of witness
> OR alternatively the length of the hearing
>
> The issues on which the Arbitrator needs to be addressed
>
> Reading aloud from documents or authorities

10.03.8.8 *Text Books/Law Reports*

> The Arbitrator to be notified if text books and/or Building Law Reports are to be referred to at the Hearing; then, 7 days before the Hearing, the party wishing to refer to such shall send the Arbitrator a copy of the complete Report or extract from the text book, with the passage on which that party wishes to place reliance suitably highlighted.

10.03.9 Advocates' Submissions

> 10.03.9.1 Opening advocates' submissions to the Arbitrator and the other party 7 days before the Hearing.
>
> 10.03.9.2 Closing submission from Respondent 7 days after close of Hearing and Claimant's submission 7 days thereafter.

11.00 Representation (s.36)

11.01 Form of representation?

11.02 Parties briefing Counsel? Consider limiting Counsel's role to that of legal expert. If so, what need for oral submissions; could all be written?

12.00 Reasoned Award

Does either party not require a reasoned award (s.52(4))?

Note: If a reasoned award is *not* required such an agreement acts as an exclusion agreement for those matters for which the parties can apply to the court for determination as set out in 13.00 below (s.45(1)).

If either party requires a reasoned award it will be requested to state where and to what extent reasons are required (in accordance with Rule 11.1, i.e. the request should include a formulation of the question(s) of law which the parties wish the Arbitrator to address).

13.00 Exclusion Agreement

13.01 Do parties wish to exclude their right of appeal on a point of law (s.69)?

13.02 Do the parties wish to exclude the right of a party to apply to the court for a determination on a question of law (s.45)?

13.03 If the parties agree to exclude their rights, as set out in 13.01 and 13.02 above, the Claimant's solicitor shall be responsible for drafting the Exclusion Agreement, the final, jointly signed version of which is to be sent to the Arbitrator.

14.00 Costs

14.01 *Security for Costs* (Rules 4.6 & 4.9)
The Arbitrator to have power to order security for costs (s.38).

14.02 *Recoverable Costs (s.63)*

14.02.1 Do the parties wish to agree what costs of the arbitration are recoverable, or leave it to the Arbitrator to determine on such basis as he sees fit, or agree that the basis shall be "reasonable amount, reasonably incurred, commercial man basis" with the Bill being in a form similar to that which a solicitor sends to his client but amplified, as necessary, to identify which fee earner was engaged on any particular piece of work?

14.02.2 Are there any aspects of the reference which the parties consider appropriate as a ceiling? **OR** is the Arbitrator to have power to limit the parties' recoverable costs? (s.65)

15.00 Inspection

If an inspection of the premises where the works have been carried out under Rule 8 is requested by the parties, or thought desirable by the Arbitrator, this will normally take place at a date to be agreed prior to the Hearing unless the parties request otherwise. On such inspection the Arbitrator will be accompanied by one representative of each party.

Alternatively, consider whether evidence should be taken on this inspection visit.

16.00 Agreement of Common Ground

The Hearing Bundle to include an Agreement as to the status of correspondence, plans, photographs, figures as figures etc. beyond those matters covered by the experts' reports.

17.00 Arbitrator's Terms and Conditions

17.01 Have Terms been signed and returned by both parties?

17.02 Interim Fee Statements—to be paid by the Claimant.

17.03 Security for Costs—usually from Claimant but also Respondent if there is a substantial counterclaim.

17.04 Once Hearing days have been reserved any party responsible for cancelling may be held liable for the Arbitrator's cancellation charges.

17.05 If settlement takes place, any Hearing days reserved shall form part of the Arbitrator's fees to be paid as part of the settlement.

18.00 Insurance

18.01 Of documents in possession of Arbitrator—consequential loss.

18.02 Of the Arbitrator in a protracted reference.

19.00 Any other business

D Mark Cato MSc FRICS FCIArb
Arbitrator

DISCUSSION ON AGENDA

The first thing to say about the agenda, I told Thomasina, concerns the note at the top: *bracketed references are to the relevant sections of the Arbitration Act 1996*. These sections are of such seminal importance that it is impossible to avoid reference to them even in the simplest of arbitrations. Indeed, as you will see, I said, not only does the AA '96 set out a number of ground rules but it makes it clear that the arbitrator has almost total freedom of action—within these ground rules—provided the parties do not agree otherwise. The Agenda is further complicated by the inclusion of references to the relatively newly introduced JCT version of the Construction Industry Model Arbitration Rules (CIMAR).

Item 1.00 Introduction

This speaks for itself, I said, except, I reminded Thomasina, that my letter to the parties, following my appointment, requested that each send along a senior representative—a decision-maker. Thus, not only do I need to know who is present at this meeting, for the purpose of my note, but also to ascertain whether or not the status of those present is likely to empower them to make decisions about any proposals I may make concerning the procedure that we should follow.

Item 2.00 Appointment

What more could I tell her about appointment? I dealt with this pretty fully in our earlier discussion (see p.11 above).

2.01 Requests the parties to produce a copy of the Notice of Arbitration. This is to ensure that any procedure laid down in the contract for giving notice to the other party that a dispute has arisen, and seeking its concurrence for the appointment of an arbitrator, has been observed.

2.02 This is sensibly inserted in the agenda so that it can be confirmed, in my Order which follows, that neither party had any valid objection to my appointment. As will be seen later, any such objection must be made timeously or the party subsequently making such objection may be deemed to have waived its right to do so (s.73 AA '96). In any event, if there is any such objection then I may rule on my substantive jurisdiction, unless the parties otherwise agree (s.30 AA '96).

2.03 Why is it necessary for the arbitrator to see the original contract? Thomasina asked. For the simple reason that he must check that the arbitration clause has not been deleted or altered and he has not been invalidly appointed, I said. She will, no doubt, recall that we discussed how this could happen when we were talking about the arbitrator's appointment, at the beginning of this exercise (see p.34 above—Item 2.03). It is for that reason that I always insist on seeing the original contract or, alternatively, if this is not available, then a certified copy.

Thomasina should note, I said, that all arbitration agreements are not formalised in contracts. AA '96 covers a wide range of possible arbitration agreements, such as an exchange of letters or an oral agreement to a standard contract containing such a clause, all of which can be effective, provided they are in writing (s.5 AA '96).

Item 3.00 *Jurisdiction* (see pp.6 and 100)

Thomasina recalled our earlier discussion about jurisdiction (see Source of Power and Authority, p.6 above), but confessed that she was still not clear about the difference between it and the arbitrator's power. I said that the best way I could illustrate this was in terms of, say, a building development. The boundaries of the developer's ownership of land could be likened to the extent of his jurisdiction—he could not, of course, build on the adjacent land which he did not own. His power could be said to be the plant that the builder employed to construct the new building. If the arbitrator determined issues outside his jurisdiction or for want of jurisdiction then he was in danger of any award that he published being set aside when he reached the end of the reference.

3.01 Challenges to the arbitrator's jurisdiction used to be a common ploy that a reluctant party might use in order to upset an Award in the event that the arbitrator's determination went against that party. AA '96 now provides against that contingency (s.30) by allowing the arbitrator to rule on his own substantive jurisdiction, and the JCT Arbitration Rules

[handwritten top margin: basically you have to object to an A's jurisdiction timeously. If you don't, you can't raise it later]

52 The preliminary meeting

give the arbitrator this power. Otherwise it requires the agreement of the parties, hence this agenda item. It does not mean, however, that his ruling is finally binding upon the parties; they can appeal his decision but they must do so timeously otherwise they can lose this right of objection (s.31). In effect, then, this section has killed off the possibility of a reluctant party using that old ploy. It is one of those device introduced by AA '96 to ensure the finality of the arbitrator's award.

3.02 If I do have to rule on my substantive jurisdiction, as set out in the two sub-sections, I told Thomasina that my preference is to deal with any objections to my jurisdiction at an early stage, possibly as a preliminary issue, in an award on jurisdiction, rather than the second option of dealing with objections in the award on the merits of the dispute.

Thomasina then, rather diffidently, asked if I could tell her what was meant by "substantive jurisdiction". For goodness sake, I said, do stop me and ask questions about anything at all you do not understand, otherwise parts of the discussion will be lost on you. Substantive jurisdiction quite simply refers to the jurisdiction that the arbitrator has to determine the substantive issues or more simply the issues in dispute, as opposed to procedural jurisdiction.

Item 4.00 Seat and applicable law

This provision of AA '96 has been included because the new Act covers both domestic and international arbitration. In the normal way, for domestic disputes, with which we are commonly concerned, it is merely a matter of confirming that the seat of the arbitration (i.e. the place where the arbitration will take place) shall be England and the applicable law shall be the law of England and Wales and Northern Ireland. Of course, in the British Isles, the law could equally be that of Scotland or of Ireland.

[handwritten margin: why is this relevant?]

Item 5.00 Commencement of the arbitration

Why is it important to confirm the commencement date of the arbitration? Thomasina asked. Charley chipped in and quite rightly said that it was to avoid an issue of limitation being raised at a later stage. Thomasina said that she did not understand what was meant

[handwritten margin: to stop prescription from running]

by limitation. I explained that there were Limitations Acts which restricted the length of time within which anyone could bring an action against another party—generally, in contract, six years. This date can vary depending upon whether the parties agreed on the appointment of the arbitrator or the appointment is made by a third party, i.e. an appointing body. However, I suggested that the level of our discussion did not warrant the further exploration of this distinction, but it was something of which, perhaps, she should be aware.

Item 6.00 *Identifying items in dispute*

Having disposed of the formalities, we now get down to the nitty-gritty, I said, and find out what this dispute is all about. I invite the parties to paint an informal picture of the dispute as they see it, adding with a smile that nothing that they say will be taken down and used in evidence etc. (Under JCT Arbitration Rules this information is supposed to be sent to the arbitrator, as soon as practicable, after appointment—Rule 6.2.)

Isn't your comment about nothing being taken down and used in evidence etc a bit flippant? Thomasina asked. No, I said. This statement, implying that they are not criminals, is deliberately inserted by me in that manner to introduce the slightest touch of humour into the situation in order to ease the inevitable tension that some people feel when involved in any judicial process. One of the most important objectives of this preliminary meeting is to instil confidence in the parties in your ability to determine this dispute fairly, and they must also realise that you are a sympathetic human being just like them. I have also found that this little joke has warmed the odd suspicious party towards me, I told her—at least that certainly has been my impression over the years. Well, she said with a laugh, I've always thought you were a funny man, but surely arbitration is a serious business. Yes, of course it is, I said, but even judges had been known to make the odd quip in the most serious of cases and, as I say, the important thing is to create the right atmosphere. However, let us move on.

First, I hear from the claimant. Sometimes—if that party is represented by a solicitor—I am handed a written summary of its case. On other occasions I hear a frank and short statement from the claimant himself.

54 The preliminary meeting

Then it is the turn of the respondent. It is not uncommon for the respondent to say that this is the first time that he really knows what the dispute is all about. In these circumstances it is not unusual for a settlement to take place shortly after, or even during an adjournment of the preliminary meeting. Assuming, however, that that does not take place, and having heard the respondent's defence to the claimant's case, I then ask the respondent if there is a counterclaim? Of course, I am not inviting the respondent to make a counterclaim, merely enquiring whether it is his intention to do so. There is usually a reason why the respondent is allegedly in breach of the contract in the first place—usually a failure to pay the claimant some money that the claimant believes is due to him. Again, what is common is that the respondent has set off or abated money due to the claimant for allegedly defective work. He may consider this to be a counterclaim, whereas strictly it is a defence. On the other hand, I said, a counterclaim is something which would stand on its own as a claim, had the claimant not started the action in the first place.

I gave her an example from my field—a dispute between a main contractor and one of his sub-contractors, where the main contractor started an action to recover money for alleged defective work and, in addition, deducted from the sub-contractor the damages for the late completion of that sub-contract (what are known as liquidated and ascertained damages). The sub-contractor, on the other hand, then made a claim (counterclaim) against the main contractor for loss and expense for having been detained on the site longer than he originally contracted for. It is clear, I told Thomasina, that in circumstances such as these the sub-contractor could have been the claimant and not the respondent and started the action against the main contractor for his claim of loss and expense for prolongation, whether or not the main contractor had started an action against the sub contractor.

Item 6.03. At this point, having noted what the issues in dispute between the parties are, I would normally discuss any such issues which I felt might not be worth pursuing, in monetary terms. Maybe, for example, I told her, there are a number of smaller issues in both the claim and the counterclaim, i.e. one could be set off against the other and thus save the parties the disproportionate cost of pursuing them. If, on the other hand, the details of the dispute are not sufficiently defined, I make it clear that, on receipt of the parties' statements, we should reconsider this possibility, i.e. keep this matter under review. Put quite simply, Thomasina, I said, although a party has the full right to pursue any legitimate claim, if the likely recovery is £100 and the cost of dealing with it in the arbitration is £200 then clearly it is better for the parties to compromise on this issue at the onset.

Anyway, I told Thomasina to note the underlined words—to keep this under constant review.

The other part of this agenda item, which suggests that one should identify and record principal areas of agreement and disagreement, is, I suggested to Thomasina, rather sanguine. It is usually far too early to make such a record.

6.04 *An agreed list of issues which remain to be determined to be handed to me not later than the close of hearing.* This is a very important direction, for it is these issues, i.e. those identified by the parties as still in dispute, which determine the arbitrator's jurisdiction in the ultimate phase—the hearing. Although my direction talks of providing this list no later than the close of the hearing, I actually prefer to receive it at the beginning. This enables me to decide on the most cost-effective way to structure the hearing and, of course, I can always amend this list and check it with the parties' representatives at the close of the hearing.

Item 7.00 Arbitrator's general powers

With this agenda item we reach the point where two schools of thought concerning arbitral procedure diverge. I belong to the school that believes in open government; lay everything on the table; make it clear to the parties (and all their representatives) just precisely what powers you have—subject to their not agreeing otherwise; everyone then knows where they stand. It is for this reason that I actually spell out the default powers I have under the Act in the absence of agreement to the contrary between the parties. (The relevant section numbers of the Act are shown on the agenda.)

The other school of arbitrators takes the view that the parties should themselves be aware of what powers the arbitrator has, in other words have sufficient familiarity with the AA '96, and if they wish to make an agreement between themselves that he should not have such powers then the initiative to make such agreement should come from them. So which school Thomasina ultimately opts for, should she become an arbitrator, must be her own choice, I told her. In any event, I suggested that we briefly consider what these default powers are.

Items 7.01.1–4

These powers are listed here because they appear like this in the CIMA Rules.

Item 7.01.5 Whether and to what extent the tribunal should itself take the initiative in ascertaining the facts and the law (s.34(2)(g))

Since the enactment of AA '96 I have not encountered one single instance of the parties attempting to restrict my powers to exercise this initiative. In other words, I have been given complete discretion over the procedure which I wished to pursue in ascertaining the facts and the law. This does not mean that I am given *carte blanche* to act as Sherlock Holmes but, in effect, it is allowing me the discretion to exercise my duty under section 33 to adopt procedures suitable to the circumstances of the case. This power also enables me to act inquisitorially. This is particularly useful if I meet with the experts outside the hearing in order to narrow the issues. This will become clearer, I told Thomasina, when we come to consider the agenda item covering experts. Charley said that this can be a particular problem in rent review arbitrations, as we will see later.

Item 7.01.6 Whether and to what extent there should be oral or written evidence or submissions (s.34(2)(h))

How a party pleads its case must depend upon the nature of the dispute and, perhaps bluntly, the amount of money in the dispute. Sometimes it is appropriate to have formal pleadings, particularly where heavyweight lawyers are involved who are familiar with this method of stating a party's case. In other instances it is perfectly satisfactory for the parties to prepare a bundle of correspondence with a short note setting out their case. Beyond these written submissions the arbitration may deem it necessary to hear oral evidence.

Although I had gently suggested to Charley that we leave his interjections until the end of our review of my preliminary meeting agenda, he could not restrain himself from saying that "documents only" arbitrations were the norm in rent review, but if they did have an oral hearing it was usually pretty short.

In my case, I said, there would be occasions when I considered that the nature of the dispute and/or the amount of money involved did not warrant the cost of any sort of hearing, and that I could also decide it on "documents only". The choice of procedure has to be viewed in the light of the arbitrator's duty to avoid "... unnecessary delay and expense", but also his duty to "act fairly and impartially as between the parties, giving each party is a reasonable opportunity of putting his case and dealing with that of his opponent ..." (s.33).

Note the words "reasonable opportunity", I said to Thomasina, not "full opportunity". This is one of the powers that the arbitrator has for restricting the amount of written or oral evidence in adopting a procedure "suitable to the circumstances of the particular case".

[margin note: A has a total power to decide documently or hearing, look at the case and be fair to the parties]

Item 7.01.7 The award of interest (s.49)

While the parties are free to agree what powers the tribunal has as regards the award of interest, in the absence of agreement the tribunal may award simple or compound interest from such dates at such rates and with such rests as it considers meet the justice of the case. This wide discretion is limited to awarding interest on amounts awarded up to the date of the award, or on any amount claimed but outstanding at the commencement of the proceedings but paid before the award was made.

Item 7.02

The first three sub-sections are default powers under AA '96, i.e. normally in the event of the parties failing to agree they are powers which the arbitrator has available to him. (Except under JCT Arbitration Rules the arbitrator has these powers and the parties are not permitted to agree otherwise.)

Item 7.02.2 Power to make a declaratory award (s.48(3))

This is simply a power for the arbitrator to make a declaration determining contested rights between the parties. For example, he may have to determine the true meaning of one of the contract clauses.

Item 7.02.3 Powers in case of a party's default (s.41(3)–(7))

These are extremely important powers which include a power to make an award dismissing the claim in the event of a party failing to attend or be represented at a hearing of which due notice was given, or, in a "documents only" arbitration, fails to submit written evidence or make a written submission (known as proceeding *ex parte*)—in each case this draconian award may only be made where a party fails to show sufficient cause for its failure. (Under JCT Arbitration Rules this must be based on formal evidence—see Rule 5.7.)

Item 7.02.4 Power to record the parties' agreement (s.5)

This section defines agreements in writing between the parties, and includes the arbitrator's record of any agreements that the parties may make, for example in respect of the powers that we are currently considering, at the preliminary meeting.

Item 7.03 The arbitrator shall have power ...

With the exception of 7.03.5 these are default powers, i.e. powers he has in the absence of agreement between the parties—but under JCT Arbitration Rules the parties do not always have this freedom to agree. It is a difference we need not explore, I said, but Thomasina should read these Rules for herself.

Item 7.03.1 Power to appoint an expert (s.37)

In the absence of agreement between the parties the arbitrator may appoint an expert, legal adviser or an assessor to assist him on technical matters.

I can understand an arbitrator needing to take legal advice from time to time, or even to appoint an assessor on a technical matter, but why should it be necessary for him to appoint an expert? asked Thomasina. You have told me that he is appointed to this dispute specifically because he has the expertise to understand the subject matter, she said.

Of course, you are right, I said, but there are frequently aspects of the dispute which are so specialised that even the arbitrator needs assistance with them. For example, in my own field computer generated networks are often produced in order to demonstrate a critical path and to justify an extension of time claim. In these cases I have found that it is most cost-effective if I appoint a tribunal expert to analyse these complex data and take me through them prior to the hearing. The parties must be given a reasonable opportunity to comment on any information or opinion or advice given by such an expert, and although this may mean engaging experts themselves I have still found this to be more cost effective than allowing the parties' own experts to argue the issue out at the full hearing. Like so many other aspects of arbitration this is a purely personal choice.

Item 7.03.2 Power to order a party to do or refrain from doing anything (s.48(5)(a))

This is a new injunctive power similar to that exercised by the courts and is a very important new power vested in the arbitrator by the AA '96.

Item 7.03.3 Power to order specific performance (s.48(5)(b))

This is a discretionary remedy by which a party, in breach of contract, is ordered to complete its performance of that contract. It will usually only be ordered by the arbitrator in the event that monetary compensation does not provide an adequate remedy.

Item 7.03.4 Power to order rectification of a deed or document (s.48(5)(c))

This power is necessary where the arbitrator finds that a written

60 The preliminary meeting

contract does not set out the true agreement between the parties and therefore needs to be amended to reflect their agreement. It can also be used where the arbitrator is satisfied that there has been misrepresentation, duress or illegality.

[margin note: how would this actually happen in reality?]

[margin note: need parties to agreement to do this]

Item 7.03.5 Power to order provisional relief (s.39)

This is a new and very important power which is only available to the arbitrator in the event that the parties are agreed. In other words it is not a default power, and therefore one on which the parties very rarely would make such an agreement. If the parties did so agree then it would enable the arbitrator to make a provisional order for the payment of money providing provisional relief to a claimant which would be subject to the arbitrator's final determination once he has heard all of the evidence. For this reason an arbitrator should exercise extreme caution before making such a provisional award.

I can understand why a claimant would be prepared to make such an agreement, but why on earth should the respondent? Thomasina asked. Surely, it would not be in his interests? I agreed that it would be a rare event were the parties to make such an agreement. However, I suggested that there could be occasions when there was a substantial counterclaim and the respondent believed that the claim itself was very weak. In this case, the respondent may well be prepared to enter into such an agreement in the hope that the arbitrator would exercise his discretion and grant some financial relief in respect of this counterclaim.

With our consideration of this last point, we had, in effect come to the end of our consideration, in this agenda, of the arbitrator's general powers under AA '96. I therefore felt that it was necessary to emphasise to Thomasina, and to Charley, that in no way could our discussion on these powers be considered to be comprehensive, particularly when they had to be read in connection with the JCT Arbitration Rules. I had deliberately simplified the issues in order not to over-complicate our discussion, but I hoped that they would appreciate, and certainly Charley should as an arbitrator's pupil, that there was no substitute for reading the Act itself or one of the first class commentaries on it.

Discussion on agenda 61

Item 8.00   Joinder/consolidation (s.35)

I told Thomasina that I was not anxious to go into the question of joinder or consolidation too deeply at this stage. It is a complex matter, I told her, and one which is possibly a little too advanced for this discussion. Having said that, I would just mention that it arises when a third party is affected by the dispute between the claimant and the respondent. A good example of this is where there is a dispute between an employer and a main contractor and a similar dispute—say, over general delay in a manufacturing process—between the main contractor and one (or more) of his sub-contractors.

In my case, of course, it is necessary to put this item on the agenda, as, if there is any possibility of joining or consolidating other disputes into the dispute to which I have been appointed, this would obviously have a serious influence on the procedure that I would adopt in the instant case. (In any event regard has to be had to Rule 3 of the JCT Arbitration Rules.)

Item 9.00   Issues (s.47)

The two sub-sections of this agenda item are an important part of the arbitrator's duty to adopt a suitable procedure and to avoid unnecessary expense. The point is that if, between them, the parties and the arbitrator can identify issues which, if resolved at an early stage, will substantially reduce the time and cost involved in preparing their respective cases, and indeed save hearing time, then the arbitrator must be alert to the possibility of taking such issues and resolving them as preliminary issues.

Item 10.00   Proceedings

At last, I said to the young, with this agenda item we are getting down to the important matter of how we should proceed in this reference. Again, I make no apology for relating this to my own field of construction, for it is that which I know best. At this point, as they will see from the agenda, we discuss whether the reference is governed by any institutional Rules, in our case the JCT Arbitration Rules, but it could equally be governed by other institutional rules.

Having heard from the parties the nature of the dispute and the amount of money involved and whether factual evidence needs to be tested by cross-examination, then, working together, the parties and the arbitrator should be well placed to be able to decide on the most appropriate procedure: whether it should be a "documents only" reference or an attended hearing; whether formal or informal pleadings or a statement of case procedure will be adopted. All these options are set out in the agenda items which follow. For our purpose, I suggested to Thomasina that we assume that the arbitrator has opted for an attended hearing, and we will examine the matters which need to be considered under that head.

Before we do so, I asked Thomasina and Charley to consider the note in parenthesis at the beginning of this agenda item. The first part of it deals with the arbitrator's duty *to adopt procedures suitable to the circumstances of the particular case* and to avoid *unnecessary delay and expense*—his important general duty under section 33 AA '96. The second part of this note deals with the parties' duty—*the parties shall do all things necessary for the proper and expeditious conduct of the arbitral proceedings*—under section 40. These two sections in turn must be read in conjunction with the overriding objective of this new Arbitration Act, set out in section 1 as follows:

> "(a) The object of arbitration is to obtain the fair resolution of disputes by an impartial tribunal without unnecessary delay or expense".

Item 10.01 Documents only

In this sub-section of the agenda, I set out the basic procedure to be followed where the parties and the arbitrator agree that the dispute is one which could reasonably be determined following a "documents only" procedure.

I pointed out the ultimate paragraph of this agenda item, which provides for the arbitrator to hear the parties on any aspect of the dispute where he considers that oral evidence is desirable or necessary for him to reach his determination.

Personally, I told Thomasina, I was not a great fan of "documents only" arbitrations. As one sage put it, "one typewriter lies as well as the next". My preference, even in the smallest of disputes, is to have some sort of physical confrontation between the arbitrator and the parties—at the least a short oral hearing. For example, I told her, there are some cases which are totally unsuitable to be determined by "documents only", namely where a brief preliminary meeting would bear fruit.

I had in mind a situation that arose in a rent review case where strong objections were registered concerning the appointment of the arbitrator by one of the parties, who felt that he (the arbitrator) could not take an objective view. In that case the arbitrator felt it sensible to meet with the parties to satisfy them on this score.

The use of a brief preliminary meeting even in "documents only" arbitrations is frequently employed, so that the arbitrator can address questions to both sides in order to clarify the issues, particularly where there is a wide divergence of opinion in the written evidence. A preliminary meeting can also unblock previously entrenched negotiating stances adopted by the parties, and thus save the often unwarranted expense of a full-blown hearing at a later stage.

The other thing to remember, I suggested, about "documents only" arbitrations is that the arbitrator will always have the choice of switching from that procedure to one more suited to the circumstances of the case. This power, of course, exists under AA '96, but also specifically under Rules where this discretion is left with the arbitrator. Thus, he may well start off believing that "documents only" is the best procedure and subsequently switch to a combination of "documents only" and, say, a short oral hearing at a later stage once he becomes familiar with the issues in dispute.

Item 10.02 Short procedure with a hearing

Although Rule 7 is peculiar to the JCT Arbitration Rules, it is an option open to the arbitrator whether or not institutional Rules apply, but, as the agenda item says, it is only suitable for quality disputes requiring a summary decision.

Item 10.03 A full procedure with a hearing

I pointed out to Thomasina that the very first item under this heading of the agenda reflects my duty to adopt procedures suitable to the circumstances of the case. "Need not all be oral", it says.

Surely, Thomasina retorted, if there are written submissions from the parties, then, the evidence is, by definition, not all oral. What I mean by introducing this at this early stage, I said, is that we must consider if, and how much of, the parties' cases can be dealt with by "documents only" to minimise the length of time occupied by the oral hearing—which, if lawyers are involved, is the most expensive phase.

Item 10.03.1   Scott Schedule (see p.141)

Is a Scott Schedule desirable? inevitably prompted the question, what is a Scott Schedule? Quite simply, I said, it was a form of scheduling groups of items of a similar nature which are in dispute, such as variations, defects etc., and comprises a series of columns identifying these specific items. There are separate columns for comments by the claimant and by the respondent, and finally one for the arbitrator. In the last right-hand side column the arbitrator records the monetary award he ultimately makes—after considering the parties' submissions—against each particular item. The total of this right-hand column then is the total quantum awarded by the arbitrator for those issues scheduled. In a simple case this can be the entire extent of the documentation. In other words, it is a very simple, and cost effective, way of pleading a straightforward case.

Item 10.03.2   Timetable

We then discussed the timetable for the delivery of the parties' written submissions. I pointed out to the young that the Rules laid down a fairly tight timescale, the objective being to get the dispute resolved as early as is reasonably possible. However, I told them, quite often I relax the recommended timescales after hearing from the parties. Of course, it all depends on the nature of the dispute and its complexity but it is important to retain a degree of flexibility and to set realistic timescales, otherwise one is faced perpetually with requests for extensions of the time; the necessity of receiving and considering comments from the other side on such applications before issuing a fresh direction all costs the parties money and therefore should be avoided if at all possible.

Although there is provision for Replies to the Defences, I asked Thomasina to note those parts of my agenda which say that the parties *shall* and those parts which say that a party *may* serve a Reply.

Item 10.03.2.7   No provision for further and better particulars (See pp.39 and 143)

[handwritten margin note: necessary if you cannot work out what the case is you have to answer]

What on earth are further and better particulars? asked Thomasina. I explained that where written submissions were concerned, they were sometimes unclear as to the point being made. The object of written submissions is that the party to whom they are being made should know the case that it has to answer. If this is not clear from the submissions then it is possible that further particulars would clarify the point, I told Thomasina. Having said that, as she could see, I make no provision for such further and better particulars, and thus the parties must be aware from the outset that their Statements of Case should be clear and comprehensive.

However, where I am prepared to receive an application for further and better particulars, I set out in this agenda the criteria which I will apply in deciding whether or not to grant such an application.

It is important that the arbitrator understands that this device, of requesting further and better particulars, <u>can be used as a delaying tactic and should be avoided if at all possible</u>. Sometimes, however, they are really necessary, in which case they should be ordered, but within a tight timescale. One thing that the young should remember, I said, is that it is commonly quoted that further and better particulars rarely live up to their name and never reveal "the Crown jewels"!

Item 10.03.3   Witness statements

Here then, I told the young, is one of those limitations on orality that I spoke about, *witness proofs of evidence are to be admitted as evidence-in-chief*. Evidence-in-chief? questioned Thomasina. Yes, I said, that's the first stage of giving evidence. I'm sure that you have seen many a play or film on the television when the lawyer asks the witness his name and where he lives, and wondered why. Well, it is first to establish that the tribunal is hearing evidence from the right person, following which that witness gives his evidence. In civil cases and in arbitration this evidence is written down and is called a proof of evidence. The arbitrator or judge will read this in advance of the hearing or the trial and as a result, and in order to save time, *[margin note top: In (A) you don't get (w) to repeat his (s) statement, you go straight in X examination]*

66 The preliminary meeting

it is taken "as read" that this witness's statement is admitted as his evidence-in-chief and, in effect, that witness goes straight in to cross-examination.

[margin: you can allow it exceptional circumstances but risky to comment by other side — again — flexibility]

I also pointed out that under this item I made it clear that I would not allow any witness to appear at the hearing who had not produced a written statement, nor, indeed, would any witness who had produced a statement be allowed to introduce new evidence. Of course, if there was good reason for allowing a new witness or fresh evidence then, having heard those reasons, and after allowing the other party to comment on them, the arbitrator should be flexible enough to modify his earlier direction.

Item 10.03.4 Experts

I reminded Thomasina that we discussed why an arbitrator—who is ostensibly an expert on the subject matter of the dispute—should wish to appoint an independent expert when we considered the arbitrator's general powers, earlier in the agenda. This present agenda item covers the situation where the parties themselves require to present part of their case through an expert, which indeed may be an issue about which the arbitrator has no expertise at all.

Having been made aware of the nature of the dispute and having heard from the parties why they require an expert for any particular issue, the arbitrator will then determine how many experts each side may call. Having done so, this agenda item lays down the procedure to be followed by these experts, including dates for the exchange of their reports, their meetings etc.

[margin: expert exchange of report prior to hearing to narrow the issues]

The latter part of this item covers the exchange of written questions between the experts following exchange of their reports. Once this exchange has been completed then it is the arbitrator's turn to ask the experts specific questions on which he requires written answers. This is a device of my own, I told the young, the intention of which is to avoid, or at least to minimise, the amount of time taken over the cross-examination of these experts at the hearing.

I also include, under item 10.03.4.7, an alternative which provides for the appointment of a tribunal-appointed expert. This is something which is favoured in the High Court, particularly in the Official Referee's Court, the idea being that, if the arbitrator appoints his own expert who advises on a particular issue, this is, or should be, cheaper than each party engaging its own expert to cover the same ground. This proposal rarely meets with the approval of the parties, who are generally not convinced of the cost effectiveness of this device. Their normal response is to say that they will require to engage an expert of their own, if only to consider the report of the independent tribunal-appointed expert. It is for this reason that I provide, under this alternative, for the parties to meet with the tribunal-appointed expert to discuss his draft report in an attempt to persuade him to amend it. In addition, I also provide the opportunity for either party who wishes to cross-examine the tribunal expert to do so at the hearing following service on me of written notice to do so, which notice must set out the matters on which the cross-examination is desired.

[margin notes: cannot × the tribunal appointed expert unless notice has been given]

Item 10.03.5 Disclosure of documents (see Discovery, p.163)

Discovery, or disclosure of documents, is a device peculiar to common law jurisdictions. It should not be necessary in a Statement of Case procedure where the parties are directed to include either copies of the principal documents on which they wish to rely, with their Statements of Case, or, at least, a list of those principal documents which the other party can then request to see.

It is for that reason that I include item 10.03.5.2, which allows either party to make an application to me in respect of any document, or class of documents, of which they are aware (or they suspect exist), that have not been disclosed with the other party's Statement of Case.

[margin notes: avoid discovery if possible ↓ too expensive]

Discovery, I pointed out, is one of the most expensive processes in the run-up to the hearing. The tradition of seeking discovery of every single document, which may or may not be relevant to the issues in dispute, most of which almost certainly will never be referred to in the hearing, is to be discouraged, I told Thomasina. I have usually found that making the party aware of the circumstances under which I would exercise my power to order specific discovery is usually sufficient to ensure that all relevant documentation is disclosed when it should be, i.e. with the parties' Statements of Case.

68 The preliminary meeting

Item 10.03.6 General

The first three items under this heading hopefully are self-explanatory. They deal with general matters concerning the service of the parties' Statements, communications with the arbitrator and applications for extensions or of time.

Item 10.03.6.4 Offers (See Costs, p.201)

I told the young that this sub-section required a little explanation. If the dispute was being heard in the High Court there was provision for paying in a sum of money as an offer to settle a claim and in the event the amount awarded by the judge did not exceed this, then the claimant (plaintiff) became responsible for paying the respondent's (defendant's) costs from the date when such offer should have been accepted.

As there is no such provision for "payments in" under arbitration the sealed offer device is employed. This means that at the commencement of the hearing the arbitrator is handed a sealed envelope. In this envelope there may be details of offers or counter-offers to settle the claim or the counterclaim, the objective being the same as the "payment in" procedure in court. Alternatively, the envelope may merely contain a blank sheet of paper.

What on earth's the point of that? asked Thomasina. Well, I said, it is thought that if the arbitrator is handed an envelope which he knows contains an offer to settle, this may be taken as an acceptance of liability of the part of the respondent. This, of course, is nonsense, I said, for anyone engaged in any form of litigation or arbitration may well consider it commercially sensible to offer to settle the matter, albeit they do not believe they have any liability. However, in view of this potential prejudice the sealed offer procedure exists if the parties wish to use it.

My own experience is that parties generally prefer to ask the arbitrator to deal with costs following his determination of the substantive issues. In this case he will not do so until after publication of his award, and it is at that stage that the parties make the arbitrator aware of the dates and amounts of any offers made, which he must then take into account when determining which party pays what costs.

I hope that's clear, I said to Thomasina, as I have greatly over-simplified what is inevitably a complex matter. At this early stage, I said, all she needs to be aware of is the possibility of a party making an offer to settle, in order to stem his liability for escalating costs. Interestingly, such offers can be made at virtually any time up to the end of a hearing, but it is axiomatic that the later they are made the less effective they are likely to be.

Item 10.03.7 Pre-hearing review (see p.167)

The item again speaks for itself. It is something that I engage in only in the larger disputes because inevitably it adds to the parties' costs.

Basically, the object is to ensure that all directions have been complied with and that no new directions are required—in effect, that the parties are, or will be, ready for the hearing by the scheduled date.

I asked Thomasina to note the underlined section in 10.03.7.1. *Are some issues not worth pursuing?* At this stage in the proceedings it will be obvious to all concerned precisely what the issues are. The amount involved in some individual items may well be far less than the cost of hearing evidence on this item at the hearing. Typically, this situation arises on Scott Schedules, for example in lists of variations or defects. I have found that by suggesting to the parties that they collect together a number of these minor items which are still in dispute, it pays them to come to some compromise on them rather than spending costly hearing time for their determination. Quite often this common sense suggestion is accepted in the spirit in which I make it.

Item 10.03.8 Hearing (see p.181)

Now we come on to the hearing itself and the arrangements for such hearing. Why only from 10.00 a.m. to 5.00 p.m., and why only four days a week? Thomasina asked. It sounds a pretty cushy number to me, she said. Not at all, I retorted. You try taking evidence for six hours a day—that is, making a hand-written note of everything that is said—and I think you'll find that 10.00 a.m. to 5.00 p.m. is quite sufficient. Indeed, some arbitrators I know only sit from 10.30 a.m. to 4.30 p.m.

Concerning the restriction to four days a week, the fifth day is necessary for the arbitrator to catch up with his other work. In my case I usually have a workload of between five and 15 references at any one time. All these are still continuing while I am sitting on another reference. There's a limit to the number of faxes I can deal with or directions that I can give in the evening or the early morning of the days that I am sitting. Thus, this fifth day, usually Friday, is the time when I try to catch up. This day also allows an opportunity for the arbitrator to review the evidence taken during the previous week and decide if there are any matters on which he requires further clarification, which he will then raise at the beginning of the following week.

Item 10.03.8.3   Venue/accommodation

My own preference for the venue is the Fleet Arbitration Centre. It is near the Law Courts and therefore situated close to barristers' chambers—which, of course, is only important when barristers are instructed. This specialist centre knows what is required and looks after me. For example, it provides a tape recording of the proceedings at absolutely no cost to the parties. A microphone is put on each of the parties' tables, one on the witness stand and one in front of me. When I come to review the evidence, if I wish to hear an exchange again it is a simple matter to select the microphone at which the evidence was being given, or the question was being addressed or put. I find this helpful when it comes to writing my award. Having said that, it is possible to hire this equipment for a relatively low cost and set it up at any venue. However, I always give the parties the opportunity of agreeing on alternative accommodation, if they can find somewhere less expensive which suits our purpose. In the absence of agreement the choice is mine.

Item 10.03.8.4   Hearing bundle

Note that I point out that the hearing bundle must be properly paginated and fully indexed. You would be amazed, I told Thomasina, how often I have arrived at a hearing to find this exercise has not been done. If there are a number of A4 files, then finding a specific document can slow down the whole hearing. If I find that the bundles have not been properly paginated, I will either adjourn right at the commencement of the hearing for this to be

[handwritten at top: not grounded and indeed ? adjourn until done or do during the lunch break]

Discussion on agenda 71

carried out or, alternatively, ask that the exercise be carried out, say, during the lunch break.

Note the second paragraph of this sub-section, telling the parties that I will wait 24 hours before reading the hearing bundle. Although I suggest that a party may have inadvertently included some "without prejudice" or privileged material in the hearing bundle, it is not unknown for this to be included deliberately in an attempt to compromise the arbitrator. It is for that reason that I give this grace period to allow both parties to review the bundle and alert me (or, more correctly, my secretary) to any offending document, which she will remove—unseen and unread by me—and return to the party which has inadvertently included it!

What do the parties wish me to read before the hearing? I ask. This is a necessary question in a large case involving volume after volume of documentation. Usually in a situation like that the parties will have agreed on a core bundle, and usually it is this core bundle which I am required to read.

Why do I need to read anything? Thomasina asked. Clearly I must familiarise myself with the general background to the dispute, I said, and the witness statements, so as to ensure that a reasonable speed is maintained at the hearing. Time spent in preparation is more than adequately compensated for by the saving of expensive hearing time.

Item 10.03.8.5 Rules of evidence

Admissibility, relevance and weight of evidence are a bit technical for a discussion at our level, I said. The basic point perhaps for Thomasina to grasp, at this stage, was the admissibility of hearsay evidence permitted now by the Civil Evidence Act 1995. Inevitably, that dear girl wanted to know more about hearsay evidence. All I would say is that it is evidence which is not first hand. That was as far as I was prepared to go, I said, on this complex subject. I had no wish to get bogged down in a discussion about hearsay evidence at this early stage.

Item 10.03.8.6 Evidence under oath

[handwritten: not required but I beola to use it]

Why is it necessary, asked Thomasina, to take evidence under oath? Quite simply, I said, it adds an air of gravitas to the proceedings.

Witnesses are made aware of the importance of the evidence that they are giving. Not every arbitrator believes that evidence should be under oath or affirmation, but I do and have always made it my practice, with, I believe, significant effect.

Item 10.03.8.7   Limitation on orality

Where there is a relatively small amount of money in dispute, in the exercise of my duty to avoid unnecessary expense it is perfectly reasonable for me to discuss with the parties the possibility of restricting the amount of time spent on cross-examination. "If, for example, we have no more than two days at our disposal, are the parties prepared to take approximately one day each in cross-examining the other party's witnesses?" is the question which I have put to them on more than one occasion. On the whole I have found that the parties are usually amenable to this sort of suggestion.

There is a natural limitation on orality with regard to examination-in-chief, I told Thomasina. She will see that when we come to discuss witnesses and their proofs of evidence, and she perhaps recalls our previous conversation when I said that I ask the parties to agree that the witness statements shall stand as evidence-in-chief, which is, in effect, a limitation on orality.

A limitation on the length of the hearing is the product of the overall objective of limiting the parties' costs. Again, depending upon the amount in dispute and the complexity and nature of the dispute, the parties are usually amenable to reasonable suggestions in this direction.

A limitation on the issues on which I need to be addressed at the hearing is also another possibility. In other words, are the parties prepared for me to determine the other issues, on which I am not addressed, purely on the basis of the written submissions that I have before me?

Item 10.03.8.8   Text books/law reports

Reading aloud from documents or authorities is something which most self-respecting arbitrators will not allow in any event, for the arbitrator is perfectly capable, or certainly should be, of scanning any document to which he is referred and indeed reading any authority placed before him where the relevant passages have been properly highlighted.

Item 10.03.9 Advocates' submissions

Where parties are represented by a trained advocate or lawyer, that person usually likes to open his party's case by summarising the issues and the evidence that he is going to bring in order to convince the arbitrator that he should find in their favour. In the past these opening submissions have been delivered orally and, in complex cases, could occupy several days. The modern method in arbitration is to have these submissions reduced in writing, and delivered to the arbitrator—copied to the other side—at least seven days prior to the commencement of the hearing, so that the arbitrator can familiarise himself with the arguments that are going be presented to him.

Similarly, at the conclusion of the hearing, these same advocates will wish to summarise the evidence that the arbitrator has heard and to reinforce the points that they made during the hearing. Thus provision is made for written closing submissions. Despite this direction, though, I told Thomasina, I have found that experienced Counsel frequently request an opportunity to make a short oral presentation to the arbitrator some time after they have presented their written submissions. This hearing usually takes place with the barristers and their supporting solicitors alone—no parties. If this oral presentation is requested then, provided the size and nature of the dispute warrants this additional expense, I will always grant the request.

Item 11.00 Representation

In arbitration the choice of the type of person to present a party's case is entirely at the discretion of that party. It could be a friend, a claims consultant, a solicitor or a barrister. The reason for asking the question at the preliminary meeting is to ascertain whether it is the intention of one party or the other to brief Counsel. If one party decides that it wishes to engage representation at this level, it is only fair that the other side has adequate warning to enable it also to brief Counsel, if that is its wish.

Having said that, there have certainly been occasions where, in discussing the case with the parties at the preliminary meeting, I have warned them that it appears to me that the dispute under consideration does not warrant engaging Counsel. Thus, while either party had the right to instruct Counsel, if it did so and my initial impression was unchanged at the end of the hearing, i.e. that the nature of the dispute did not warrant such heavyweight representation, then I would consider disallowing the cost of Counsel as a recoverable cost under the arbitration.

How can you do this? asked Thomasina. I understood that costs were dealt with by a taxing master in the High Court? First of all, I said, there is provision under AA '96 for me to *determine* the parties' costs (s.63)—that is the new expression for taxing those costs. I always make it my business to undertake this task to ensure early finality to the dispute. In any event, even if I'd decided that the case was so complicated that it warranted being determined (taxed) by a Taxing Master, I could still influence his decision by marking my award "Not Fit for Counsel".

What's this business about limiting Counsel's role to that of legal expert, asked Thomasina? Well, I said, it is an idea of my own which has yet to find favour with Counsel. As I see it, certainly in the smaller cases, most of the issues are probably technical, although there may well be one or two legal points which need arguing. Why not then limit Counsel's role to that of a legal expert, i.e. to assist the tribunal to understand the law? This would have the undoubted advantage of keeping the overall costs to manageable levels. It may well be that, under AA '96, an arbitrator could direct that Counsel's role be limited to that of a legal expert or, alternatively, if either party decided to use Counsel in a wider role then a substantial element of counsel's fees would be disallowed.

Item 12.00 Reasoned award (see p.187)

I assume that a reasoned award is just that, an award with reasons, said Thomasina. But why would either party *not* require such an award? she asked.

Under the old legislation, I said, one party or the other had to request that the arbitrator produce a reasoned award or he had no duty to do so. Under the new Act the situation is reversed; the arbitrator must produce a reasoned award unless both parties agree that one is not required.

This is a delicate subject, as you can see from my agenda, I said. In this item I am positively suggesting to the parties that they may *not* require a reasoned award. My object in including this on the agenda is that in some of the smaller cases, frankly, the cost of a reasoned award is not warranted.

Why should it cost any more? asked Thomasina.

I told her that I believe that the same point was made by the committee drafting this new legislation. Undoubtedly it takes longer to write a reasoned award than one without reasons, even if the latter is in sufficient detail so that each party knows why it won or lost on a particular issue—which, I believe, is the minimum that any award should cover. My view is confirmed by Lord Mustill— the doyen of the arbitration world—who has written the definitive work on the subject. He says "The preparation of all well drafted reasoned awards involves a great deal of work..." (p.374—2nd edn).

I know that I said at the beginning of this conversation that it seemed self-evident what a reasoned award was. Now I'm not so sure, said Thomasina.

I am not surprised, I said, for this is something which has exercised the minds of the best lawyers in the land. For the best definition I know, I can do no better than to quote Lord Goff from a shipping case in 1981, when he said:

"A reasoned award need not take any particular form; although a typical form of reasoned award is one in which the arbitrator, having set the general scene and identified the dispute between the parties, then sets out the parties' respective contentions, makes any further findings of fact which may be desirable for the purpose of considering those contentions and then sets out his conclusions and reasons for reaching that conclusion. In such an Award facts found by the arbitrator appear to form an inseparable part of the total reasons for his Award."

I could not resist also quoting my favourite judge, whose judgments have given me the greatest pleasure: that excellent storyteller, Lord Denning. He explained his thinking behind his judgments as follows:

"I'd tried to make my judgment live—so that it can be readily understood ... I start my judgment, as it were, with a prologue—to introduce the story. Then I go on from act to act as Shakespeare does—each with its scenes— drawn from real life ... I draw the characters as they truly are—using their real names ... I avoid long sentences like the plague: because they lead to obscurity. It is no good if the hearers cannot follow them. I strive to be clear at all costs. Not ambiguous or prevaricating. I refer sometimes to

76 The preliminary meeting

previous authorities—I have to do so—because I know that people are prone not to accept my views unless they have support from the books ... But never at much length. Only a sentence or two. I avoid all references to pleadings and orders—they are mere lawyers' stuff—they are unintelligible to anyone else. I finish with a conclusion—an epilogue—again, as the chorus does in Shakespeare. In the end I gather the threads together and give the result."

Lord Denning makes it sound easy and rather fun, said Thomasina. Well, I said, you must remember that a reasoned award is not quite the same as a judgment. However, there is much good advice to be had from Lord Denning's explanation.

As we are in danger of getting into too much detail over what is, after all, meant to be a superficial overview of arbitration, I suggest we move on. Having said that, I said that I hoped Thomasina appreciated that the whole business of reasoned award was a substantial subject of its own.

to guarantee finality if no appeal.

Item 13.00   Exclusion agreement (see pp.177 and 209)

This item is fairly self-explanatory, I said. If both parties agree that they do not require a reasoned award then that automatically excludes their right of appeal to the court on that award or, indeed, the right to apply to the court to determine a question of law.

can appeal to crt to determine a point of law.

Why would the parties, or a party, be prepared to exclude their rights? asked Thomasina. Surely any sensible person would keep all of its options open? she said.

The point about entering into an exclusion agreement, I said, was that in doing so the parties are guaranteed finality to the dispute. Alternatively, the fact that by keeping the possibility open one or other of the parties may be able to appeal the award on a point of law—albeit today on very narrow grounds—means that neither party can be absolutely certain that the end of the arbitration will mean that the dispute will finally be resolved.

I told the young that I had actually been in the situation where the parties agreed to enter into an agreement excluding all of their rights of appeal to the court, but still required a reasoned award. One of the parties in that case was a local authority and, I believe, needed a fully reasoned award to justify to the Audit Commission the cost of having pursued the dispute to arbitration.

So basically, if there is no reasoned award, then there is no right to appeal, even on a point of law.

if parties agree for the bt not to order claimant to provide security for costs, remember to nonetheless request security for the (A)'s costs (respondent's)

Item 14.00   Costs

Item 14.01   Security for costs (s.38(3)) (see p.157)

The power to order the claimant to provide security for the costs of the arbitration is one of those default powers, i.e. one that the arbitrator has unless the parties have agreed otherwise. Strictly then, I said, the arbitrator does not have to ask the parties if he is to have this power. In my case I prefer to lay my cards on the table and give the parties the opportunity of coming to an agreement, if they so wish, that I shall *not* have such power. Interestingly, I cannot recall one instance, since the enactment of AA '96, when the parties have made such an agreement under this section.

The other thing to remember about security for costs under this section, I told the young, was that the costs of the arbitration include the arbitrator's costs. Thus, if by some obscure chance the parties made an agreement under section 38, I have made provision under my terms and conditions to allow me to request security for my fees and expenses despite not having a general power to order the claimant to provide security for the respondent's costs. (See clause 8 of those Terms—p.81.)

Item 14.02   Recoverable costs (see p.201)

14.02.1   AA '96 has given the arbitrator power to limit a winning party's recoverable costs under two heads. This first one concerns the determination of what costs a party may recover at the end of the arbitration (s.63)—basically *reasonable costs reasonably incurred*. But, as I mentioned earlier to the young, it is possible to warn the parties of any amounts that you may disallow; for example, as I suggested previously, counsel's fees in a case which I considered did not warrant the employment of a barrister.

14.02.2   The other area in which the arbitrator has some control over the parties' costs (provided the parties have not agreed otherwise) is a limitation on the total cost of the arbitration or any part thereof (s.65). This is a matter which I tend to discuss with the parties at the preliminary meeting, in order to ascertain their views and—provided the parties do not agree, as has happened on more than one occasion, that it is inappropriate for me to impose a limit, or ceiling, on their costs—then I explain that I will receive

[margin: LIMITATION OF COSTS]
[margin top: cost m/s be reasonable cost, reasonably incurred — can limit total cost and make it a % of the amount at stake.]

78 The preliminary meeting

submissions from them and make a decision whether or not to exercise my discretion to limit their costs, once I have had the opportunity of studying the Defence. Any decision prior to this exchange of pleadings I consider is premature.

I told Thomasina that I had taken some trouble to explain this business of costs to her for, as she will no doubt learn, costs are a very important aspect of arbitration. Prior to the enactment of AA '96, costs had escalated to a point where there was very little to choose between arbitration and litigation in the courts. With the new Act and the new power it vested in arbitration, in the right hands arbitration has been brought back much closer to its original roots; that is, a flexible form of dispute resolution tailored to the nature of the dispute and not hidebound by traditional court methods. As a result, using this flexibility of procedure, good arbitrators have been able to bring the cost of such actions back to a sensible percentage of the amount at stake between the parties.

[margin: % of amount at stake]

Item 15.00 Inspection

[margin note: ok but accompanied by a rep from each party.]

This item speaks for itself. Sometimes it is thought desirable for the arbitrator to carry out a site inspection, for example in a construction dispute where there are alleged defects or, in a commodity dispute, an inspection of the goods which are the subject of the dispute.

I asked Thomasina to note that, in the normal way, the arbitrator should be accompanied by a representative from each side whose job it is to point out what it is they want him to note. Normally, the arbitrator will not take evidence from either representative during a site visit, but there is absolutely no reason why he should not do so, provided he has warned the parties that is his intention, and it makes sense to do so in the circumstances of the case.

[margin: can take evidence during site visit but warn parties first.]

Item 16.00 Agreement on common ground

[margin note: agreement incl in the bundle to prevent time wasted]

This is another item which speaks for itself. It is clearly important that the arbitrator is aware of the extent of common ground between the parties. Directing that the parties prepare an agreement covering common ground and include it with the hearing bundle is one way of ensuring that time is not wasted at the hearing in establishing facts which would be readily admitted, as well as a way of narrowing the issues. (See also Notice to Admit Facts, p.149).

Item 17.00   Arbitrator's Terms and Conditions

I asked the young to note particularly that I leave my own terms to be discussed as one of the last items on my agenda. A number of arbitrators I know make this the first item on their agendas. If the parties are not agreed on their Terms and Conditions then they refuse to proceed any further. This, I believe, is very bad psychology. While there is no real need for the parties to agree the arbitrator's Terms and Conditions—as they are, in any event, jointly and severally liable for his reasonable fees (s.28)—it is clearly more satisfactory if the parties do sign and return a copy of these terms and conditions to the arbitrator.

In the case of appointments made by the RICS, the arbitrator is appointed without the parties having the opportunity of agreeing or disagreeing his Terms and Conditions, thus their liability is only to pay *reasonable* fees, in the event that they do not contract otherwise by both signing his Terms and Conditions.

Why then, asked Thomasina, should it be necessary, or even desirable, for the parties to sign your Terms? Well, I said, let's look at those Terms.

ARBITRATOR'S TERMS

WHEREAS a dispute has arisen between Reliable Builders Ltd. and Sanctuary House Ltd over Works at Sanctuary House, Woodbridge, Suffolk.

The Parties to the contract hereby agree to submit all disputes and differences arising out of and in connection with the contract between the Parties for the above Works, to be referred to arbitration under the Arbitration Act 1996 and to the arbitration and final decision of a person to be nominated by the President, or a Vice-President, of the Royal Institution of Chartered Surveyors and on the nomination of the said President, or Vice-President, as such we have jointly agreed to the appointment of

D MARK CATO MSc FRICS FCIArb

as the said Arbitrator

We hereby jointly and severally agree as follows:

(1) A minimum non-returnable commitment fee of £XXX plus Value Added Tax will be paid by the Claimant forthwith; this amount to be set off against fees and expenses, otherwise payable under this Schedule, should such fees and expenses equal or exceed the amount of this minimum fee.

(2) To pay the fees and expenses of the Arbitrator at the rate of £YYY per hour (charged at one minute increments unless subject to a minimum period as specified herein) for all time engaged upon the duties of the reference, other than the Hearing (irrespective of whether the matter reaches a Hearing or Award) together with all expenses, disbursements and outgoings incurred by him. For the avoidance of doubt expenses, disbursements and outgoings covers, inter alia, typing charges, photocopying, faxing, telephone, travel and subsistence. The hourly rate will be subject to review annually on 1 January and is likely to be increased roughly in line with the annual level of inflation reported in the previous December.

(3) To pay the fees and expenses of the Arbitrator at the rate of £YYY per hour, for time spent at the Hearing or Interlocutory Meetings, with a minimum charged per day (for Interlocutory Meetings) of £ZZZ.

(4) Where the Arbitrator travels inter-city, air or rail, travel

shall be first class; where on suburban routes, second class, unless it is a hearing day (which usually means travelling in the rush hour) in which case, this too will be first class. Travel time, other than that spent reading in connection with this arbitration, will be charged at half of the above quoted hourly rate.

(5) Once dates for a Hearing or Interlocutory Meeting have been fixed, a fee shall be payable for time set aside and not spent, calculated as a percentage of the time charge set out above, according to the period of notice before the first day fixed for the Hearing or meeting as follows:

More than 180 days	Nil
Between 90 days and 180 days	25%
Between 30 days and 90 days	50%
Between seven days and 30 days	75%
Seven days or less after commencement of the Hearing	100%

If the period fixed for the Hearing exceeds 20 working days the fees payable for time set aside and not spent, as set out above, shall be further reduced by the following percentages, counting from the first day fixed for the Hearing or from the date of cancellation, whichever is later:

From 21st to 30th day	25%
From 31st day to 52nd day	50%
From 53rd day onward	75%

For the avoidance of doubt, set aside days are charged at 8 hours per day and include pre-hearing reading & preparation and post-hearing collation and award drafting days, unless agreed otherwise, roughly equivalent to 25% of the days set aside with a maximum of seven days at either end.

(6) All fees and expenses to be subject to the addition of Value Added Tax at the appropriate rate.

(7) The Arbitrator may deliver interim fee notes quarterly and these are payable by the Claimant, 14 days after delivery, unless otherwise directed. Interest will be charged, on any fees remaining unpaid 14 days after delivery, at the rate of 5% p.a. above NatWest base rate monthly rests.

(8) Even if the Parties have made an agreement under s.38(3) of the Arbitration Act the Arbitrator will still retain the power to order security for his own fees and expenses.

82 The preliminary meeting

In such an eventuality the Parties shall lodge such security in respect of the Arbitrator's fees and expenses as he may, in his absolute discretion, direct and it is clearly understood that this money belongs to the Arbitrator. However, should it subsequently transpire, at the completion of the reference, the Arbitrator is not beneficially entitled to the entire sum paid as security, then the overpayment will be refunded and a credit note issued.

(Note: Security will normally be required to be deposited by the Claimant—subject to an appropriate contribution from the Respondent, as the Arbitrator may direct, should there be a Counterclaim of substance—in the full amount of the fee payable in respect of any Hearing upon dates for that Hearing being firmly fixed).

(9) Where the parties have made no agreement under s.65 of the Arbitration Act 1996, in respect of the Arbitrator's power to limit the recoverable costs of the arbitration, for the avoidance of doubt, unless specifically directed by the Arbitrator, any limit subsequently imposed by him, after receiving and considering submissions from the parties, will relate to the *parties'* recoverable costs only, not those of the Arbitrator as referred to in s.64 of the Arbitration Act 1996.

(10) Any money paid in advance as fees and expenses will be placed in the Arbitrator's normal bank account and any interest earned thereon will accrue for the benefit of the Arbitrator.

(11) All outstanding fees are payable on taking up the Award or ten days after notification that the Award is ready for collection, whichever is earlier.

(12) In the event of a settlement of the issues by agreement between the Parties before an Award is made, the fees and expenses properly payable to the Arbitrator shall be paid by the Party or Parties responsible for doing so under the Terms of Settlement, within 10 working days, after notification of the amount irrespective of whether a Consent Award is required or published.

For the avoidance of doubt, should the responsible Party fail to pay these fees and expenses, both Parties remain jointly and severally liable for them.

(13) The Arbitrator will be entitled to make time charges up

to the settlement of his Final Fee Claim which, for the avoidance of doubt, may include any time, including court time, spent chasing fees.

(14) Any costs incurred by the Arbitrator in connection with any power given to him under the Arbitration Act 1996 will be deemed to be part of the Arbitrator's fees and expenses.

(15) In the event that the Arbitrator is empowered under s.37 of the Arbitration Act 1996 to take legal or technical advice,
The Arbitrator will
  (i) discuss with the Parties the choice of legal or technical advice
  (ii) show the Parties the advice received or tell them the substance of the advice if given orally, and
  (iii) give the parties the opportunity of addressing him briefly upon it, if they so wish, before he finally decides the point (as provided for in s.37(1)(b) of the Arbitration Act 1996).

(16) This Agreement is not effective until it is signed on behalf of both Claimant and Respondent.

Agreed by/on behalf of the Claimant	Agreed by/on behalf of the Respondent
....	....
Status	Status ....
Date..................	Date.................

84 The preliminary meeting

The first thing, I told the young, to note about these terms is that, if signed by both parties, they could constitute a written arbitration agreement. This could be useful in the event that there was a subsequent dispute over my jurisdiction.

Moving down the first page, we see that the parties agree to be jointly and severally bound by the terms. This forenote is not strictly necessary for, as I said earlier, the Act makes it quite clear that the parties are jointly and severally liable for the arbitrator's *reasonable* fees (s.28). This, though, goes further than mere agreement as to what is a reasonable level of fees. For example, (1) calls for a minimum non-returnable commitment fee (which, if it was not included in a written agreement between the parties, could be considered to be *unreasonable*); (2) makes it clear that disbursements are excluded from the hourly rate and spells out what those disbursements comprise. This clause also gives the arbitrator the right unilaterally to increase his fees on 1 January each year.

How can an arbitrator decide unilaterally what his new charging rate will be? said Thomasina. Surely he has to agree this each year with the parties, she said. I have operated these terms and conditions for very many years and at the beginning of January each year have informed the parties what is my new charging rate, I said.

Not once has a party questioned the new rate. However, if they did, and they were to consider it to be unreasonable, then they would be protected by the Act. (Their redress is to apply to have those fees settled by the court—s.28.)

(3) allows me to make a minimum charge for any interlocutory meeting. Of course, I have discretion not to levy this charge if for some reason I am able to share the time spent attending an interlocutory meeting with some other business. However, any meeting usually means travelling to and from London, plus the time spent at the meeting, in effect losing at least one half of the day.

(4) I asked Thomasina to note that all travel time is charged at 50 per cent of my hourly rate unless it is spent reading or drafting.

(5) deals with the controversial issue of cancellation charges. Why should you be able to get a cancellation fee, Thomasina said, when barristers and solicitors cannot? The reason is quite simple, I said. Barristers work from chambers where a clerk is usually ready to hand them another brief if the case they are working on settles or is adjourned. In other words, a successful barrister will always have

Discussion on agenda

a flow of work, but an arbitrator, on the other hand, should not take on more work than he can deal with expeditiously. Indeed, this is an undertaking that I give for all of the appointments made by the RICS.

I asked the young to note that my cancellation charges were well graduated. Nothing if the hearing is cancelled more than six months from when it was scheduled to begin, down to 100 per cent of the fee that I would normally earn on days set aside should the case settle or the hearing dates be postponed for any reason, within seven days of the commencement of that hearing. I even grade these cancellation charges down further where the length of the hearing exceeds 20 days.

I also drew their attention to the time I set aside, both before the hearing for preparation and for reading, and post-hearing for drafting the award. I could not stress too strongly how important it is that the arbitrator is as familiar as he can reasonably be before he sits at a hearing. During this preparation period I frequently draft all of the recitals to the award; the background to the dispute; what is being claimed and, if applicable, the counterclaim. Through this device I am not only well prepared when I attend the hearing, but I also have a flying start with the award once the hearing is over. I have no patience with arbitrators who take several months to prepare an award following the conclusion of the hearing. In my case I rarely take more than seven to 10 days.

(7) This term allows me to deliver quarterly fee notes—although I don't often bother, I said—but more importantly it allows me to charge interest at a fairly punitive level on any fees remaining unpaid 14 days after delivery of the fee statement. Surprisingly, on the few occasions when I have found it necessary to charge interest, the parties have usually paid up without demur.

(8) Here then we have the clause that I mentioned when we discussed security for the parties' costs. This enables me to ask the parties for security for my fees, even if they do not give me power to call for security from the claimant for the respondent's costs.

(9) This is an important clause. The reason is that the Act makes no distinction between the arbitrator's costs and the parties' costs. Thus, if an arbitrator imposed a limit on the parties' recoverable costs without such a term, he could find that he had inadvertently limited his own fees, which, under the circumstances, as he has little control over the amount of time that the parties take in

complying with his directions and thus probably increased the time that he spent on the reference, would penalise him unfairly.

(10) This term is included in order to avoid the problem of maintaining a separate client account. As I never ask for money in advance to which I would be entitled should the case settle or the hearing dates be postponed, then it is not unreasonable that any interest earned on money deposited with me, for security for my fees, be paid to my account.

(13) I include this item to enable me to continue charging the parties for my time should I be forced to pursue them jointly for my fees following settlement, or the conclusion of the hearing, if they remain unpaid.

(14) This term reinforces what the Act says about the arbitrator being able to recover disbursements incurred on behalf of the parties in exercising his powers to appoint a tribunal, legal assessor or adviser.

(15) I include details here concerning the consultation process which I will go through in the event that I do exercise my power to take legal or technical advice under section 37 AA '96.

(16) This final clause makes it clear that the agreement is not effective until it is signed by both parties. In other words the arbitrator is not able to make an agreement with one party only.

Having been through my terms and conditions in some detail I said that I hoped that the young understood why I found them to be an important tool in running the arbitration. They certainly gave me more power to control matters than I would have otherwise.

How often do parties resist signing these terms? asked Thomasina. I could honestly say that in over 100 appointments there had only been two occasions when the respondent refused to sign these terms. On those occasions, I had said, so be it. As the parties are bound to pay me reasonable fees and the charging rates that I had informed them about from these terms were certainly reasonable, I had no difficulty in proceeding without their being signed. (See also Fees And How To Get Them Paid, p.175.)

Item 18.00   Insurance

I added this final clause to the agenda following an accident which occurred some time ago, when I was travelling back from a hearing. The car caught fire and a small portion of my notes, which I had taken during the hearing, were destroyed. It resulted in witnesses having to be recalled briefly and the lawyers and I reconstructing the evidence that was lost from their notes. This exercise added to the parties' costs and although I waived my own charges for this work the parties were undoubtedy out of pocket. Having had this experience, it seemed to be sensible at least to alert the parties to the possibility of taking out a single premium insurance policy, particularly in very large cases which may go on for several weeks. Although this suggestion does not get taken up very frequently, at least I make it.

Of course, I said, it's not only the documents which are at risk, hence the need for the second part of this agenda item. I recalled a story concerning an elderly arbitrator who was sitting on a long case. Towards the end he found it necessary to adjourn as he felt unwell. It transpired that he was suffering from heart trouble. The parties, although naturally very concerned about the arbitrator himself, were also worried that he might not make it to the end and be able to produce his award. This would mean possibly starting again or at least covering a lot of the ground a second time with a new arbitrator. For this reason, again if there is a substantial sum involved and the case is likely to last several weeks, I offer the parties the possibility of insuring my life for the period up to the date when I should have completed my award. As I am usually in rude health, the parties usually laugh this one off, but it is a serious suggestion which they ignore at their peril!

Item 19.00 *Any other business*

That's it, apart from any other business, I said. In fact it is rare for the parties to raise any new matters at this late stage, as the agenda is pretty comprehensive and should have covered almost every conceivable point. However, one must still give each party the opportunity of raising any issues which it would like discussed. I usually go round a table looking, not only to the parties' representatives but to the principals of the parties themselves. This is one of those very rare occasions when they may address the arbitrator informally and one which should not be lost.

Well, said Thomasina, that was jolly interesting. I must say that I had absolutely no idea how complicated this arbitration business really is; you're quite a clever old thing really!

It's not really that complicated, I retorted. It is just that my personal style is to cover a lot of ground at the early stage. I believe that by doing so and setting the tone and the pattern of the reference from day one, the arbitrator has a far firmer control over the proceedings and is therefore more easily fitted to discharge the duty imposed upon him by the Act—*to avoid unnecessary delay and expense.*

That's all very well, Thomasina said, but how long do these so called preliminary meetings last? We must have spent a good three hours discussing the agenda. I agreed that it had taken some time but that a normal period for such a preliminary meeting varied between one and 2 hours. If the parties were represented by solicitors, what frequently happened was that they would produce written comments on the agenda, which would have been sent to them at least a week or so before the meeting. Where there was agreement, little or no discussion was necessary.

OK, said Thomasina, you've covered a lot of ground, how do you ensure that there is no confusion about what you have agreed? Quite simply, I said, by producing an Order for Directions. Perhaps you would like to see a copy of a typical Order that I would produce following such a preliminary meeting?

Oh dear, said Thomasina, my dear godfather, I really don't think I could take any more today. I promise you, I really did find what you had to say really interesting and want to hear more. From what you have told me I am not at all daunted at the prospect of becoming an arbitrator. Of course, not for many years, she said, obviously not wishing to give offence to my grey hairs. I can see that it could be a demanding but fulfilling occupation.

I laughed and agreed that I thought we had covered a lot of ground and apologised to Charley who I knew had wanted to tell us about his parallel experience in rent review. I offered to give them dinner in the near future and continue our discussion on that occasion. They accepted with alacrity and left.

A week or so later, after a good supper, we sat down over our coffee and I produced the Order for Directions which I promised I would run through with them.

ORDER FOR DIRECTIONS

IN THE MATTER OF THE ARBITRATION ACT 1996

and

IN THE MATTER OF AN ARBITRATION UNDER THE JCT 1998 EDITION OF THE CONSTRUCTION INDUSTRY MODEL ARBITRATION RULES

between

RELIABLE BUILDERS LTD   **Claimant**

and

SANCTUARY HOUSE LTD   **Respondent**

ORDER FOR DIRECTIONS NO 2

(Note: All bracketed references are to the relevant section of the Arbitration Act 1996 and THIS DIRECTION IS AN AGREEMENT IN SO FAR AS THE MATTERS SET OUT HEREIN ARE EXPRESSED TO BE "BY CONSENT" IS AN AGREEMENT IN WRITING, PURSUANT TO s.5 OF THAT ACT).

UPON hearing Representatives for both Parties on 11 November 1998 the following Directions are given by CONSENT (unless otherwise noted) and it is HEREBY DIRECTED that:

1.00 Parties

The **Parties** in this Arbitration are

1.01 Reliable Builders Ltd
Snape Yard
Woodbridge
Suffolk   as **Claimant**

1.02 Sanctuary House Ltd
Registered Office
Matthews House
Main Street
Ipswich
Suffolk   as **Respondent**

2.00 Appointment

The parties agree that I have been validly appointed (s.16(1)).

3.00 Jurisdiction

I may rule on my own substantive jurisdiction (s.30). However, both parties confirmed that I had jurisdiction to determine all dispute and differences arising out of, and in connection with, the contract between the parties, which is the subject of this reference.

4.00 Seat and Applicable Law

The seat of the arbitration shall be England (s.3) and the applicable law shall be the law of England and Wales (s.46).

5.00 Commencement of the Arbitration

The commencement date for the arbitration is 22 August 1998, the date on which the claimant wrote to the respondent requesting the appointment of an arbitrator (s.14(5)).

[handwritten margin note: when you write and ask for an arbitrator to be appointed, that is the commencement date for purposes of prescription]

6.00 Contract

The contract governing this dispute is the JCT Intermediate Form (IFC 84) as Amended.

7.00 Arbitrator's General Powers

7.01 Procedural and evidential matters
The parties make no agreement as to procedural and evidential matters under s.34, thus leaving it to my discretion to decide on all such matters, which for the avoidance of doubt, is not limited in any way by specific references to this section elsewhere in this Direction.

7.02 It shall be for the Arbitrator to decide:

  7.02.1 The extent to which he shall take the initiative in ascertaining the facts and the law (s.34(2)(g)).

  7.02.2 Whether and to what extent there should be oral or written evidence or submissions (s.34(2)(h)).

  7.02.3 On the award of interest (s.49(2)–(5)).

7.03 The Arbitrator shall have

    7.03.1 Power to make a declaratory award (s.48(3)).

    7.03.2 Powers as set out in s.41(3)–(7) in case of party's default.

    7.03.3 Authority to record any agreement reached at the Preliminary Meeting on behalf of the parties (s.5).

7.04 The Arbitrator shall have power to:

    7.04.1 Appoint Experts (including a tribunal appointed expert, if agreed; to take legal advice or appoint an assessor (s.37).

        7.04.1.1 Should I wish to invoke this power I will first submit the name of the proposed appointee to the parties who may object on reasonable grounds; however, the final decision will be mine.

        7.04.1.2 Any opinion received from any expert or legal adviser appointed by me shall be in writing and copied to the parties, who will be given a reasonable opportunity to make their own submissions to me on it (s.37(1)(b)).

    7.04.2 Order a party to do or refrain from doing anything (s.48(5)(a)).

    7.04.3 Order specific performance of a contract (other than a contract relating to land) (s.45(5)(b)).

    7.04.4 Order the rectification, setting aside or cancellation of a deed or other document s.45(5)(c)).

    7.04.5 To correct awards or make additional awards, namely...

    S.57(3)(a)/s.57(4) to (6) of the Act apply to these proceedings.

8.00 Conduct of the reference

    8.01 JCT 1998 Construction Industry Model Arbitration Rules apply.

    8.02 Statement of Case—Rule 9 procedure.

9.00 Preliminary issues

There were no preliminary issues which it was considered could be conveniently dealt with at a separate hearing but this matter will be reviewed following service of the Statement of Case.

10.00 Timetable

10.01 The Timetable for service of Statements/Submissions is to be as follows:

10.02 The Statement of Case from the Claimant to be delivered to me and to the Respondent no later than 5.00 p.m., 10 December 1998.

10.03 The Statement of Defence and Counterclaim (if any) to be delivered to me and to the Claimant not later than 5.00 p.m., 28 days after service of the Statement of Case.

10.04 A Statement of Reply to the Defence may be delivered to me, and the Respondent, not later than 5.00 p.m., 14 days after service of the Statement of Defence.

10.05 All Statements shall set out the factual and legal basis relied upon and shall include a list of any documents the Claimant or Respondent considers necessary to support any part of the relevant Statement and a copy of the principal documents on which reliance will be placed, identifying clearly in each document the relevant part or parts on which reliance will be placed.

10.06 The Claimant's Statement of Case shall incorporate a Scott Schedule with full particulars of each item in dispute separately listed.
The Respondent will complete his part of this Schedule with his Defence.

10.07 Any applications for an extension of time must be made to me, in writing, before the time directed expires—copied to the other side.

10.08 For the purpose of calculating dates the 9 days between and including 23rd December 1998 and 2nd January 1999 shall be ignored.

11.00 Service

11.01 Statements may be served by facsimile, first class

post, DX or courier, but if by facsimile then a hard copy must follow by first class post. If the Statement itself is sent by facsimile with the supporting documentation following, then the facsimile will be considered good service.

11.02 If either party fails to comply with the timetable set out above, the other party to notify me of non-service or late service.

12.00 *Counsel (s.36)*

The Respondent intends to instruct Counsel and the Claimant reserves his position (s.36).

13.00 *Experts*

13.01 Each party is given leave to call one Expert. The parties will attempt to agree on joint instructions. A copy of the agreed instruction to be sent to me or, if no agreement, details of those points of instruction on which they do agree and details of those on which they do not.

13.02 These instructions to state whether Experts will meet "open" or "without prejudice" and also what authority they have (if any) to bind their respective parties. In any event privilege shall be waived for any matter agreed at these meetings.

13.03 The Experts are to meet not later than 28 days after the service of the last Statement or satisfactory Reply to any Request for Further and Better Particulars thereof. (See 10.03.5.7 Agenda for the Preliminary Meeting.)

13.04 The Experts shall endeavour to narrow the issues and to agree facts as facts, figures as figures etc. as far as possible.

13.05 They shall prepare, date and sign a note of the facts and opinions upon which they are agreed and of the issues upon which they are not, copy of such note to be exchanged and delivered to me no later than 14 days before the hearing.

14.00 *Disclosure of documents*

14.01 There is no provision for general disclosure of documents under this procedure as documents on which parties wish to rely will be disclosed and included with their Statements.

14.02 However, if one party can satisfy me that the other party is likely to have in his power or possession documents which might be helpful to that party's case or damaging to the other party's case which are not included with the supporting documentation of that party's case then, provided I am satisfied of the relevance of the documents, I will initially invite voluntary disclosure, in default of which I will order selective disclosure (Rule 5.2/s.34(2)(d)).

14.03 In addition to those documents disclosed and included with the parties' Statements, each party shall append, to its initial Statement, a list of all other documents in their possession or power, under main category headings, which may be relevant to the issues in dispute.

14.04 Inspection of any documents listed in 14.03 above, or the subject of an application under 14.02 above, to be given on 3 working days notice.

15.00 Hearing

15.01 After the word "shall", in the first line of Rule 9.41, the words "unless otherwise directed" are added.

15.02 There shall be a **Hearing** in this Arbitration for which two hearing days have been reserved, 12th and 13th July 1999.

15.03 Each sitting day will be from 10.00 a.m. to 5.00 p.m. with one hour's recess for luncheon.

15.04 The Hearing shall be held at suitable accommodation arranged by the Claimant with the agreement of the Respondent. If the parties cannot agree then the Claimant shall book accommodation at the Fleet Arbitration Centre, 6th Floor, Hulton House, 161–166 Fleet Street, London EC4Y 2DY. Telephone 0171 936 3111 (s.34(2)(a)).

15.05 Exchanged proofs of evidence shall be admitted as evidence in chief.

15.06 All evidence shall be on oath or affirmation (s.38(5)).

15.07 The strict rules of evidence as to admissibility, relevance and weight shall not apply subject to reasonable objection (s.34(1)(f)).

15.08 An agreed list of issues which remain to be determined to be handed to me not later than the commencement of the hearing.

15.09 Should either party be responsible for the postponement or cancellation, without good cause, of the Hearing days set aside then that party will be responsible for the costs thrown away by that postponement or cancellation.

16.00 Agreed bundle

16.01 There will be an **Agreed Bundle** for the Hearing. It will be the Claimant's responsibility to ensure that this Bundle is properly paginated and annotated and a copy delivered to me no later than 7 working days before the hearing.

16.02 The parties require me to read this bundle.

17.00 Proofs of evidence

17.01 Proofs of evidence, of witnesses of fact, to be exchanged and a copy delivered to me no later than 6 weeks after the service of the last Statement or satisfactory Reply to any Request for Further and Better Particulars and to be admitted as evidence in chief but a brief examination in chief will be permitted if requested.

17.02 Except by my leave (which will only be given in special circumstances), no witness may be called at the Hearing unless a written proof of evidence has been provided in accordance with the preceding paragraph. No further evidence in chief may be adduced by a witness on any matter which has not been included in that witness's proof of evidence either specifically or by reference to a document or documents listed or produced in accordance with Direction 10.05 above.

17.03 All Statements, together with their supporting documentation served under these Rules shall, once proved, be admitted as documentary evidence.

96 The preliminary meeting

18.00 Common ground

An agreement as to the status of correspondence, plans, photographs and figures as figures etc beyond those matters covered by the experts' reports shall be included in the Agreed Bundle.

19.00 Law reports/authorities

Seven days before the Hearing the parties will provide me with complete copies of any additional Law Reports or authorities not included in their Statements on which they wish to rely with the appropriate passage/passages suitably highlighted.

20.00 Advocates' submissions

20.01 Advocates' opening submissions shall be reduced to writing and delivered to me and the other party at least 7 days before the Hearing.

20.02 Advocates' closing submissions shall be reduced to writing. The Respondent's advocate's closing submissions to be delivered to me and the other party not later than 7 days after the close of the Hearing and the Claimant's advocate's closing submissions to me and the other party not later than 7 days thereafter.

[handwritten margin note: award 10 days after receipt of report]

21.00 Awards

21.01 The Claimant requires a reasoned award (s.52(2)).

21.02 Accordingly, the Claimant shall set out in writing to me a formulation of the question(s) of law on which that party might wish to appeal.

21.03 I may make an award including some or all of the following remedies (and only those remedies), namely
...
S.48(3)/s.48(4)/s.48(5) of the Act do apply to these proceedings.

22.00 Costs

22.01 *Security for costs*
I am to have power to order security for costs (s.38(3)).

22.02 *Recoverable costs (s.65)*
I shall have the power to direct that the recoverable

costs of these proceedings or any part of them be limited to a specified amount. I shall consider exercising this power following the receipt of the Statement of Defence and counterclaim (if any), when I shall invite written submissions from the parties, on the matter.

22.03 *Settling the parties' costs (s.63)*
The recoverable costs are to be determined by me at my discretion, if not agreed, on a "reasonable amount, reasonably incurred, commercial man basis" with the Bill being in a form similar to that which a solicitor sends to his client but amplified, as necessary, to identify which fee earner was engaged on any particular piece of work.
The procedure for this determination of costs will be the subject of a separate direction following the publication of the award on the substantive issues.

23.00 Court's powers

23.01 *To enforce peremptory orders* (s.42)
The court shall not have the power to require any party to comply with any peremptory order made by me in these proceedings pursuant to s.41(5) of the Act, and s.42 of the Act shall not apply to these proceedings.

23.02 *In support of proceedings generally* (s.44)
For the purposes of and in relation to these proceedings, the court shall not have the power to make orders about the matter[s] listed in s.44(2)(a)/(b)/(c)/(d)/(e) of the Act.

24.00 Communications

All communications to me to be in writing (not by telephone) copied to the other party and may be sent by facsimile, in which case a further copy must be sent forthwith by first class post.

IT IS FURTHER DIRECTED THAT:
25.00 I may submit quarterly Interim Fee Accounts in accordance with my Terms and Conditions in which case these will be paid by the Claimant. I shall exercise the discretion I have by virtue of Clause 8 of my

Terms and require Security for my Fees and Expenses, in such sum as I shall direct, one month before the Hearing.

26.00 As the Hearing days listed above are now reserved, should either party be responsible for cancelling or postponing them, then that party may be held liable for costs thrown away and, in particular, my cancellation charges as set out in my Terms and Conditions.

Similarly, should these Hearing days be abandoned as a result of a settlement between the parties, such cancellation charges shall form part of my fees to be paid by the parties as part of the settlement.

27.00 Costs in the Reference.

28.00 Liberty to apply.

Date: 12 November 1998	**D Mark Cato MSc FRICS FCIArb Arbitrator**
To: Reliable Builders Ltd	**Representative for the Claimant FAO Harry Hocking**
Sanctuary House Ltd	**For the Respondent FAO William Bliss**

Having given a copy of this typical order for directions to Thomasina and Charley, I took them through it briefly, as I had promised, skipping those items which were obvious or with which we had dealt fully when discussing the agenda.

I pointed out that the note at the beginning of the order was included with the express purpose of recording those directions which were expressed be "By Consent" and that my order constituted an agreement in writing under s.5 AA '96. Thus, unless a party objected, within a reasonable time of the receipt of this order, to any part of that direction, they could find themselves estopped from lodging such objection at a later stage (s.73).

DISCUSSION ON ORDER FOR DIRECTIONS

Item 1.00   Parties (see Introduction, p.50)

I start by defining who are the parties to the arbitration. I know that this may seem rather obvious, I said, but, from my own personal experience, there have been occasions when in the past a party has been defined incorrectly—it may, for example, be a subsidiary of a large group—and the holding company's name is given as a party instead of that of the subsidiary company, which is in fact the party to the contract. That would result in reference being conducted in the wrong party's name and any award which resulted, referring to that wrong party, would be a nullity and the whole process could have been wasted. For this reason it is obvious, I said, but one must be clear who are the correct parties. If there is an error, then by listing the parties in this Order an early opportunity is given to either side to correct it, and thus to avoid abortive expense.

Item 2.00   Appointment (see pp.11 and 50)

This was dealt with fully when we discussed the agenda. Here, this merely records that both parties accept that the arbitrator has been validly appointed—a classic example of where the parties will lose an opportunity to object unless such objection is made timeously.

Item 3.00   Jurisdiction (see pp.6 and 51)

Again, this is an issue which we aired fully when discussing the agenda. This item records the parties' agreement that I may rule on my own substantive jurisdiction should it be necessary. However, it goes on to confirm that the parties agree that I have full jurisdiction to deal with all of the disputes and defences which have been referred to me.

Item 7.00   Arbitrator's general powers (see p.55)

Here it will be seen that the parties made no agreement as to procedural and evidential matters, and thus left it entirely to my discretion, allowing me complete freedom to adopt procedures suitable to the circumstances of the case, within the constraints of natural justice and even-handedness as set out in section 33 AA '96.

The remainder of this item records those default powers which I have by virtue of the fact that the parties have declined to make any agreement. Why bother? said Thomasina. For the simple reason, I said, that I included them on the agenda in the first place. I like the parties to know precisely what powers I have, so that when, and if, I come to exercise all or any of them at a later stage it comes as no surprise to them.

Item 11.00   Service

Note, I said, 11.02. Here I make the parties responsible for informing me of non-service or late service in compliance with my directions. The reason for this is that at any one time I could have a dozen or so references running and it would be a tedious administrative task to keep track of when I had directed that a particular statement or document should be served, particularly as a number of these will be subject to extensions of time from the original Order for Directions. It is therefore preferable that the parties themselves keep an eye on the timetable and inform me when the other party is in default.

Item 22.00   Costs (see pp.77, 157 and 201)

It will be seen from this item that I have power to order security for costs and power to direct that the recoverable costs (usually those of the winning party) will be limited to a specified amount. Importantly I confirm when I will consider exercising this power, *viz. following the receipt of the statement of defence and counterclaim (if any)*, and only then following consideration of written submissions from the parties.

Items 26.00–28.00   Further directions

These four final items are under the heading of IT IS FURTHER DIRECTED THAT, as none of them is clearly "By Consent".

If the rest of this direction was not crystal clear then I have not done my job properly, I told the young. What it does, in effect, is to lay out before the parties, or the representatives, the procedure for the entire reference, up to and including the hearing. As I said earlier, setting the hearing dates at a reasonable distance ahead focuses the minds of the parties wonderfully. It certainly can influence the number and extent of any interlocutory applications that they may wish to make between the preliminary meeting and the scheduled hearing.

Having got thus far, and Charley having exercised a laudable degree of patience, I suggested that this would be a good moment for him to explain briefly the differences between my approach and his, or rather his pupil master's, in rent review disputes. I had long suspected that we follow quite different procedures in running our arbitrations and I was soon to find out the truth of that belief.

CHAPTER 6

RENT REVIEW ARBITRATIONS

Charley started by pointing out that he knew of no instance of a rent review arbitration being subject to any particular Rules except perhaps one possibly in connection with agricultural holdings, where the reviewed rent is subject to the Agricultural Holdings Act 1986, which lays down its own procedure.

It is quite common, he said, for rent review disputes to be resolved very soon after the appointment of the arbitrator, the appointment itself often precipitating settlement. Recognising this, and to avoid abortive costs, many rent review arbitrators' first letter after appointment, while inviting the parties to agree on the procedure for the resolution of their dispute, defers the date for the holding of a preliminary meeting (unless the parties agree that one is not required) for three to four weeks to allow both parties to request further time for negotiations. Charley produced a model letter which is used by his pupil master.

MODEL LETTER

Sir/Madam,

**In the matter of the Arbitration Act 1996
and in the matter of an arbitration between
—— (the Landlord) and
—— (the Tenant)
Property: ——**

I have been appointed as **Arbitrator** by the President of the Royal Institution of Chartered Surveyors (RICS), in the above dispute, by appointment dated ... to determine the rent of the above property.

1. **Lease:** the RICS has sent to me a copy of the above Lease dated ... made between ... (1) and ... (2). If either party wishes to verify the authenticity of the documents I have in my possession, on request I will send both parties a copy.

I am told (by the RICS) that you have received a copy of the Case Details from which my appointment derives. Please confirm that these details are correct.

2. **Parties:** please confirm to me the correct full names and addresses of the parties to this arbitration. If either party is to be represented then the name and address of that representative to whom I shall address all future communications as if that representative were the party.

3. **Procedure:** this arbitration is governed by the Arbitration Act 1996 ("the Act").

The stated objective of this Act is to obtain a fair resolution of the dispute without unnecessary delay or expense. The parties are free to agree the procedure for resolving the dispute, subject to each party having a reasonable opportunity of putting their case and dealing with that of their opponent.

You may agree jointly any procedural or evidential matter. Such agreement must be in writing. If it is helpful I will provide a document for completion for such agreement.

Matters on which you could agree include amongst other things: the timetable and venue for meetings/hearings; the type of documents to be exchanged between you and delivered to me; the type of documents which shall be disclosed between you; questions you may ask each other in the procedure (as opposed to questions at a hearing); the type of evidence introduced and when; whether to have a hearing.

For example: at the one extreme there could be a full oral hearing exchange of written statements of case; discovery; exchange of witness statements with the strict rules of evidence applying; at the other extreme I could, with your agreement, decide the dispute according to the principles of equity and fair dealing—sec. 46. "equity clause".

If you do not jointly agree the procedure and evidential matters I have the power to decide them after I have considered matters disclosed to me bearing in mind my duty to adopt procedures suitable to the circumstances of the case.

4. **Issue of law:** when replying please let me know whether or not there appears to be any dispute on the interpretation of the Lease or on any other legal matter.

5. **Preliminary Meeting:** I intend holding a Preliminary Meeting in this reference to consider, and hopefully agree amongst other things, procedural and evidential matters, on one of the following dates to suit both parties ... at a venue to be agreed between the parties or if not agreed at ...
UNLESS (a) both parties agree that a Preliminary Meeting is not necessary, and
   (b) the parties agree on the procedure to be followed (as set out above), or
   (c) I hear in the meantime that the dispute has been settled.
When I learn whether or not a Preliminary Meeting is to be held I will issue a further Direction either
   (a) confirming the date, time and venue, together with an Agenda for this Preliminary Meeting, or
   (b) setting out a Draft Direction for the parties' consideration, which comments will be taken into account before issuing this as a firm Direction.

6. **Resolution of the dispute:** if, at any stage, the parties reach a settlement the parties should notify me immediately. Any settlement should be comprehensive to include all matters referred to arbitration and should include agreement as to who is to pay my fees and expenses (apportioned if appropriate).

I should also be informed whether or not the parties wish me to publish an Agreed Award encapsulating their terms of settlement. If so, a copy of those terms, signed by both parties, should be sent to me with the request.

7. **Acknowledgement/communications:** Please acknowledge receipt of this letter. All communications to me should

be in writing **with confirmation that a copy has been sent simultaneously to the opposing party**.

For the avoidance of doubt, it is not necessary for copies of all correspondence between the parties to be sent to me.

Please note that no "without prejudice" correspondence or negotiations shall be disclosed to me, including any opening shot if without prejudice privilege is expressly reserved. For the avoidance of doubt I regard any part of a bona fide negotiation for a settlement, whether or not marked "without prejudice", as privileged and inadmissible unless the privilege has been expressly and unambiguously removed. **I stress the importance of this direction.**

8. **Fees:** my fees will be on the based on an hourly rate of £ ... calculated upon the time I spend on the reference. Disbursements/expenses will be charged in addition to cover such matters as typing, DX, faxes, postage, photocopying, room hire, legal advice (if appropriate) and other relevant expenses. The hourly charge and the disbursements are both subject to the addition of VAT.

If the matter proceeds on written submission only, with or without a preliminary meeting, I *estimate* my time involvement is unlikely to produce total fees, ex VAT, exceeding £ ... for my declaratory award as to the amount of the rent.

I stress that this is only an estimate on the assumption that there are no unusual circumstances, interlocutory issues or issues of law to be resolved requiring significant time involvement.

The parties will appreciate that if there is to be a hearing, it will only be possible for me to estimate my total costs when I have received and considered the parties' Statements and I know the length of the hearing.

9. **Applications:** either party may apply to me in respect of any matter in this letter. However, I request the parties, in respect of this application or one being made to me in the future, to first liaise with the opposing party and then if there is agreement I will issue an Agreed order. If no agreement is reached then I will invite the non-applicant party to comment before I issue a direction; this will take time and may add to costs.

Yours faithfully,

[*Arbitrator*]

DISTRIBUTION:

As we saw from this letter, if both parties do not request an adjournment or agree on a procedure which does not include a preliminary meeting within the time limit imposed, the arbitrator will, of course, proceed. Rent review arbitrators, like any other arbitrators, are under a duty to tailor the procedures to suit the case, Charley said.

I suppose that the most interesting difference between the rent review arbitrator's approach, in this instance, and my own is the built-in delays in proceeding with the reference, to enable the parties to negotiate a settlement, should they so wish. This option, of course, is always open but in this case the rent review arbitrator positively invites the parties to attempt to settle before they get embroiled in the arbitration. The other interesting aspect of this letter concerns the arbitrator's fees and his estimate of his total fee provided the matter proceeds on written submissions only. Charley said that they were sufficiently experienced to know pretty well how much time a dispute would take to resolve by "documents only" and therefore were able, with some degree of confidence, to give a typical estimate of their fees—something I would not personally like to do in a construction arbitration or, at least, not at this very early stage.

Many rent disputes, we were told, proceed solely on written representations and, in smaller cases, where the amount of rent in dispute is low, parties often dispense with a preliminary meeting. Quite right, I said, observing the arbitrator's duty to adopt a procedure suitable to the circumstances of the case. With an eye on costs, rent review arbitrators, in such circumstances, rarely impose too formal a procedure, certainly not against the parties' wishes for informality.

With this in mind, Charley then showed us the letter they send convening a preliminary meeting, when there is no agreement on procedure. Attached to this letter were comprehensive notes for guidance for the parties. Charley claimed that this "friendly accommodating approach" at such an early stage concentrates the minds of the parties while making it clear that the arbitrator controls the procedure!

DIRECTION FOR PRELIMINARY MEETING

Sir/Madam,
**In the matter of the Arbitration Act 1996
and in the matter of an Arbitration between
—— (the Landlord) and
—— (the Tenant)
Property ——**

1. I acknowledge receipt of ... letter dated ... confirming that no agreement has been reached on the procedure to be followed in this reference. Although the parties have agreed on ... 1998 for this meeting, no agreement has been reached as the venue. ACCORDINGLY I DIRECT THAT a preliminary meeting will be held at ... on ...

2. I enclose an Agenda for this meeting which should be read in conjunction with my previous letter in which I set out various alternatives which we can discuss at the Preliminary Meeting.

If I either party intends to be represented by a solicitor or barrister, they are to inform me, and the other party, in advance of the Meeting.

I attach hereto Notes for Guidance for the parties to consider in advance of the Preliminary Meeting. These Notes are particularly relevant where the dispute is to be resolved by written submissions only.

Both parties should acknowledge this letter, which, for the avoidance of doubt, can be taken as my Order for Directions No.1.

3. If the person(s) attending the Preliminary Meeting is a representative of a party please ensure that that representative has the authority of the party to agree relevant matters on that party's behalf.

4. At the Preliminary Meeting, I shall not receive evidence of any kind in respect of the matters in dispute. This meeting is to determine the procedural and evidential matters generally.

5. If either party/representative fails to appear at the Preliminary Meeting without reasonable cause, within half an hour from the commencement time, I shall adjourn the meeting, to a date to be notified. In practice I hope that in the event of "last minute problems" the party in difficulty would endeavour to contact both me and the opposing party.

Yours faithfully,

[*Arbitrator*]

DISTRIBUTION:

NOTES FOR GUIDANCE FOR THE PARTIES.

1. **General:** I shall ensure that each party be given a fair opportunity to present its case and to know and meet the opposing case. At all times I shall be conscious of the primary objective of the 1996 Act, which is to give the parties the right to agree how their dispute is to be resolved fairly, without unnecessary delay or expense.

2. **Statement of Case, Reply to Statement of Case:** it is for the parties to tell me their case; I am expected to receive the evidence of witnesses and submissions and to be guided by them in reaching my conclusion. With this in mind I shall not draw inferential conclusions if there is no evidence to support such a conclusion.

I may not rely only on my expertise unless and until I have given each party the opportunity of commenting on it.

The parties should be aware that if a party's submission/evidence is not contested by the opposing party I shall regard such submission/evidence as accepted unless it falls short of establishing the contention in support of which it is made.

3. **Evidence:** I shall weigh the evidence for each party against the factual material put before me. In so far as there is no factual material on the evidence in question I will test the evidence against the relevant experience of the witness and the manner in which that experience and the evidence stand up to contradiction.

If a party wishes to introduce evidence by affidavit, I and the other party shall be informed in advance.

4. **Reasons:** under the act the parties are entitled to a fully reasoned award. However, in order to avoid unnecessary delay and expense, the parties should consider limiting the extent that they require reasons, e.g. solely the calculation from which the amount of the rent is derived, the weight attached to each (or the most helpful) comparable introduced, issues of law etc.

5. **Inspections:** I shall indicate to the parties a convenient date for my inspection. At my inspection I shall not receive evidence of any kind save that each party/representative may draw my attention to factual matters referred to in evidence. For the avoidance of doubt what I see at the inspection shall be evidence; what I hear shall not be evidence. The parties shall inform me not later than the stage of service of reply to statements

of case if they wish to accompany me during the inspection. If the parties agree that I shall make my inspection unattended and if one of the parties/an employee is in occupation of the subject premises I infer I have approval of the opposing party for me to inspect in the presence of the occupant. I shall not inspect in the presence of one party's representative without securing from the other agreement to that effect.

I shall wish to inspect the subject property in detail. If either party wishes me to inspect any of the comparable properties introduced in detail, I am to be advised and I shall expect that party to make the necessary arrangements for my inspection. If no request is made to me to make a detailed inspection of a comparable property I shall look at such areas of it as may be regarded as "public areas" normally seen by visitors to the property.

6. **Partial award:** in the absence of an application by either party for a partial award (an award with matters reserved) I shall, subject to my discretion, publish an award final on all matters except on recoverable costs (a party's costs), if not agreed.

I remind the parties of the possible merit, in appropriate circumstances, of a partial award in respect of one or more of the issues (but not all of the issues) within the dispute if such a partial award would be likely to achieve an expeditious and cost effective resolution of the dispute.

7. **Costs generally:** I am bound by the provisions of the Act to include in my award (or further award, as the case may be, if costs are not agreed) my decision as to how costs of the arbitration are to be borne.

Costs include the legal or other costs of the parties; the fees and expenses of any arbitral instruction concerned (if appropriate); as well as my fees and expenses. It is nevertheless open for the parties to agree a division on costs; in which case their agreement should be included in an agreed statement.

I remind the parties of the relevance of special circumstances in the exercise of my discretion, e.g. a valid *Calderbank* offer. In the event of any offer upon which a party intends to rely in my discretion on costs no such offer shall be communicated to me until matters other than costs have been resolved. If, however, a sealed offer procedure is intended I will, on application, issue directions.

If the amount of the winning party's recoverable costs cannot be agreed between the parties then I will determine the amount, following a further direction on the procedure which I will adopt for such determination.

8. **Points of law:** if an issue of law arises at any stage in this reference, I remind the parties that, unless otherwise agreed by both parties, I may appoint a legal adviser or assessor, whose costs will become part of the costs of the arbitration. In this event I shall give the parties a reasonable opportunity to comment on any information, opinion or advice obtained by any such person.

9. **Discovery:** I will give no order for general discovery. However, if one party can satisfy me that the other party is likely to have in his possession, or power, documents which might be helpful to that party's case or damaging to that other party's case, which are not included with the supporting documentation of that party's case then, provided I am satisfied of the relevance of the documents, I will initially invite voluntary disclosure, in default of which I will order specific discovery.

Thomasina chipped in at this point to say that as a rent review arbitrator knows precisely what the dispute is all about from the papers sent to him on his appointment, is not a preliminary meeting in any event an unnecessary expense, particularly if the reference is to be "documents only", and in view of what I had said earlier about the arbitrator's duty under section 33 to avoid such unnecessary expense?

Not so, Charley said. His pupil master takes the view that there is great merit in a preliminary meeting. Indeed, much as I do myself, I said. Much can be achieved, especially if the parties are not represented or their expert representatives are inexperienced in arbitration work which, alas, can often be the case.

In rent review disputes, the occasion of the preliminary meeting may well be the first time that the party itself has been involved in arbitration and that party may not be aware of what the dispute is really all about. Charley's pupil master, we were told, has found that by explaining to such parties what arbitration is and how it works, fears and anxieties can be allayed, confidence created, confusion avoided and settlement encouraged.

The arbitrator thus satisfies himself that the parties understand what is going on and what is expected of them. As a result he will be able to assess quickly the degree of gravitas that will be appropriate; often a source of criticism if the parties have not met the arbitrator.

It is important that the arbitration service should be perceived as user-friendly. Any suggestion of being too distant, authoritative, patronising, flippant or incompetent can be overcome easily by holding a preliminary meeting. Anyway, that is what Charley and his pupil master think, we were told. All very laudable, I said.

What could I say about this second letter, other than it demonstrates a quite different approach from my own? Certainly the notes for guidance cover a number of the matters which I would expect to discuss at the preliminary meeting with the parties or their representatives. However, I can see some merit in the rent review arbitrator's approach, but couldn't help wondering if Charley's pupil master doesn't go over the top slightly in discussing how he intends to weigh the evidence, for example.

Having established that a comparatively lower level of formality was more often than not adopted in rent review arbitrations, Charley then produced a typical agenda which they use for their Preliminary Meetings.

AGENDA FOR PRELIMINARY MEETING

IN THE MATTER OF THE ARBITRATION ACT 1996
AND IN THE MATTER OF A RENT REVIEW ARBITRATION
RE: [property]
—— (LANDLORD)
—— (TENANT)

PRELIMINARY MEETING AGENDA

1. **Confirmation:** of correct names and addresses of parties; of Claimant, Respondent; of authenticity of copy documents submitted; of any additional documents.

2. **Jurisdiction:**

3. **Formulation of disputed matters:** identification of issues within the dispute.

4. **Agreed statement of facts:** in particular: floor areas, improvements, comparable properties intend to be relied upon. ? to be included in Statement of Case.

5. **Methods of representations:**
   (i) *Procedure for a hearing*: either
      (a) Pleadings, Further and Better Particulars, Discovery, Inspection; or Statement of Case (skeleton or full exposition)/Reply thereto.
      (b) Advocate, lay advocate, written openings and closings, written summary of issues.
      (c) Witnesses, expert witnesses, sequential/simultaneous exchange of statements in like disciplines and meetings.
      (d) At hearing: Oath/Affirmation: sec.38(5); Transcript/shorthand note of the hearing.
   (ii) *Procedure solely on written submissions*: exchange and delivery of
      (a) Schedule of comparables intended to be relied upon,
      (b) Agreed statement of facts (? included in Statement of Case),
      (c) Statement of Case,
      (d) Reply to Statement of Case,
      (e) Summary of contentions. Meetings of experts.
   (iii) Agreement to an "equity clause".

6. **Timetable:**
7. **Resolution of issues of law:** ? appointment of experts or legal advisers—sec.37.
8. **Discovery:** Sec.34(2)(d).
9. **Evidence:** Sec.34(2)(f).
10. **Inspection:** Sec.38(4)(a).
11. **Unreasoned award:** Excludes applications to court—sec.45 & sec.69.
12. **Interest:**
13. **Awards on different issues:**
14. **Copies of authorities intended to be relied upon:** recognised full report required.
15. **Completion of representations:**
16. **Resolution of dispute:** sec.51(5) on costs.
17. **Costs**
    Of the arbitration: sec.59. Allocation—sec.61(1)(2). Recoverable costs—sec.63.
    Determination of recoverable costs: sec.63.
18. **Applications generally:** parties should try to seek agreement first.
19. **Other matters:** any matters arising from the Notes for Guidance not covered elsewhere in this agenda.

Date:

ARBITRATOR   Distribution:

There was little that I could say about this agenda other than that it served to demonstrate a different approach to my own. I produce a very full agenda—17 pages in all—whereas this agenda occupied only one and a half pages. However, as it appears to be used regularly by a very experienced rent review arbitrator, and it works, it shows that there is no right or wrong way of running an arbitration.

PLEADINGS

Charley then told us about their approach to "pleadings".

In rent reviews, Charley said, to state the obvious, the dispute is the amount of the rent, and their view is that as this is clearly known to the parties there is no "cause of action". As a result they claim that formal pleadings are rarely appropriate as they would achieve very little—there are no facts to allege. In some circumstances formal pleadings may be appropriate but the arbitrator should be satisfied that this is the best route before ordering pleadings. This is not often the case and therefore the Statement of Case route is nearly always adopted.

Having said that, Charley said that his pupil master was only too aware that a Statement of Case can mean different things to different individuals—e.g. should it be a full Statement of Case with all witness statements (fact and expert) and legal authorities annexed, or is it to be in skeletal form with further submissions reserved? Are witness statements to be in skeletal form or in the form of a proof of evidence?

Having explained to the parties how the Statement of Case procedure works, apparently they always canvass the parties' views before deciding on the precise procedure to be adopted, assuming that the parties have made no agreement on procedure under section 34 AA '96—which Charley said had never happened in their experience since the new Act came into force.

For example, he said, if there is to be a hearing, the parties may or may not wish to have the opportunity to deliver a Reply to the Statement of Case. Natural justice, of course, dictates that the party requesting the opportunity to deliver a Reply should be given that opportunity. The procedure at the hearing and the arbitrator's discretion are, of course, no different from that in any other form of arbitration.

If it is a "documents only" procedure the Statement of Case is usually prepared by the party's valuer representative to which he will attach any legal submissions. By necessity it must be a full Statement of Case followed by a Reply, he said.

We were interested to hear that it is not unusual for parties to deliver their submissions in duplicate to the arbitrator, leaving him to effect the exchange. Fortunately, this quaint custom has not permeated into the construction arbitration world. On a practical point, Charley said that if the arbitrator effects exchange he should make it clear to the parties that he will not look at the documents delivered until three days after that exchange, thus allowing a party to object to any offending materials. I told Charley that we also follow a similar procedure, usually when the agreed bundle for the hearing is delivered.

Evidence adduced in a rent review dispute nearly always includes references to comparable transactions. In rent review arbitrations much apparently is said about questions of relevance and admissibility of transactions. Charley said that his pupil master tries to persuade the parties to sort out any differences themselves; that is, agreeing on directions and hopefully avoiding the costs of a legal assessor or obtaining Counsel's opinion. If admissibility is contested on crucial relevant evidence then, of course, he addresses and determines the issue. However, it is often the case that the contested evidence is only a part of the whole evidence. In such circumstances, Charley's pupil master reminds the parties that it is the arbitrator who decides the quality of the evidence and the weight to be attached to it and will often resolve their differences over admissibility.

In rent review arbitrations, as in construction arbitrations, provided the parties have made no agreement to the contrary, it is at the arbitrator's discretion to what extent to apply the strict rules of evidence. Authority requires the arbitrator to deal with all the evidence, including uncontested evidence (as to admissibility), that may be technically inadmissible (e.g. a previous rent award on a comparable property).

Charley told us that to give the parties an equal opportunity to make submissions, whether at a hearing or on "documents only", it is not unusual for them to order that, prior to Statements of Case, the parties exchange a list of comparable transactions on which they intend to rely. Such lists are to include as much factual information relating to those transactions as possible. Each party's Statement of Case can then address all the comparable evidence introduced.

Charley said that his pupil master also recommends the practice, in a "documents only" procedure, of ordering the parties to prepare a "summary of contentions" to be exchanged and delivered after replies to Statements of Case. He stressed that this was not a current general practice with rent review arbitrators, but his pupil master thought it had the merit of concentrating the parties' minds on identifying the issues within the dispute. Usually the summary of contentions is limited to, say, two sides of paper. A further useful benefit accruing from this summary is that it provides a skeleton for the arbitrator for his reasoned award. With this in mind, as he is obliged to give a reasoned award, unless both parties have agreed otherwise, on issues of facts, Charley says that they think it a good idea, in appropriate cases, to tell the parties that reasons will be limited to those matters identified in the summary of contentions, thus ensuring that all matters upon which either party places reliance have been dealt with.

Charley then showed us model directions which they issue following their preliminary meeting, where there is to be a hearing.

Order for directions on "documents only" after preliminary meeting

ORDER FOR DIRECTIONS ON DOCUMENTS ONLY
AFTER A PRELIMINARY MEETING

IN THE MATTER OF THE ARBITRATION ACT 1996
AND IN THE MATTER OF AN ARBITRATION BETWEEN

—— (THE CLAIMANT)
AND
—— (THE RESPONDENT)

ORDER FOR DIRECTIONS NO: ...
Upon hearing the parties/representatives at a preliminary meeting held on ... and upon considering their submissions [Upon receiving procedural submissions without a preliminary meeting]

I HEREBY ORDER AND DIRECT BY CONSENT THAT:

1. **Parties:** the landlord shall be the Claimant and the Tenant shall be the Respondent.

2. **Conduct of the case:** the representative having conduct of a party's case should comply with this order as if it were the party.

3. **Arbitration by documents only:** the arbitration shall be on documents only with written representations with liberty to either party to apply for a hearing.

4. **Hearing:** I reserve the right to call a hearing if, within my discretion, I consider it appropriate.

5. **Evidence:** the strict rules of evidence shall not apply.

6. **Comparables:** any comparable transactions intended to be referred to in either party's statement of case shall be delivered to the opposing party on or before ... [date] with simultaneous delivery to me. Any such comparable transactions shall include as many facts as possible relating thereto and, in particular, floor areas and plans (if any).

7. **Statement of Case:** each party shall prepare a Statement of Case, being a full presentation of the case, to be exchanged simultaneously, in duplicate, by the parties not later than fourteen days after delivery of comparables with subsequent delivery to me.

8. **Agreed facts:** as many facts as possible relevant to my

award as to the amount of the rental value of the subject property shall be agreed between the parties and their agreement recorded and included within the parties' statement of case.

9. **Reply to Statement of Case:** any reply to the opposing party's Statement of Case shall be exchanged simultaneously, in duplicate, by the parties not later than 14 days after exchange of Statements of Case with subsequent delivery to me.

10. **Summary of contentions:** each party shall prepare a written summary of its main contentions, being a résumé of the case in an abbreviated form not exceeding three sides of A4 paper. The summary shall be delivered simultaneously, in duplicate, to the opposing party not later than ten days after exchange of the reply to statement of case with subsequent delivery to me.

11. **Contents of Statement of Case:** a party's statement of case shall be made by a named person and should include:
    The correct name and address of the claimant respondent.
    Identification of all of the issues within the dispute upon which a party places reliance and the contentions thereon;
    Documentary evidence (if any) including statements of witnesses of fact and/or expert witnesses (if any) upon which a party places reliance;
    Propositions of law (if any) upon which a party places reliance;
    An honest rental valuation of the subject property together with valuation calculations upon which it is based; a statement setting out the valuation assumptions on the basis of which the valuation has been made; analyses of comparable transactions (which are admitted).

12. **Contents of Reply to Statement of Case:** replies shall not include any evidence other than evidence in rebuttal of the opposing party's statement of case and they should not introduce evidence on new matters.

13. **Issue of law:** if an issue of law arises the other party must be informed of its subject matter in advance to allow the other party full opportunity to respond. The parties/representatives shall formulate any question(s) of law in writing in a form suitable for inclusion in my award.

14. **Evidence:** in the event of a party intending to introduce

evidence by affidavit the other party must be informed in advance.

15. **Without prejudice meetings:** (1) at a time convenient to the parties, before exchange of Statements of Case, the parties/their experts shall hold a without prejudice meeting or discussion to identify those matters upon which they are agreed and not agreed. They should prepare a list of those matters upon which they are agreed and, if possible, those matters on which they are not agreed for inclusion in their statement of case.

    (2) At a time convenient to the parties after exchange of Reply to Statement of Case and before exchange of summaries of contentions, the parties/their experts shall hold a without prejudice meeting or discussion to attempt to narrow the issues and identify the issues to be included in each party's summary of contentions.

16. **Confirmation of without prejudice meetings:** within three days of completion of the meetings the parties/experts shall confirm to me that the meetings I direct in para.15 have taken place.

17. **Communications:** all communications to me shall be in writing and shall be copied to the opposing party and contain confirmation that a copy has been sent simultaneously to the opposing party.

18. **Inspection:** inspection by me of the subject property shall be allowed at a date to be arranged.

19. **Acknowledgement:** parties to acknowledge receipt of this Order.

20. **Costs:** costs of the preliminary meeting and this Order are costs in the arbitration.

21. Liberty is given to either party to apply.

DATE:

ARBITRATOR

DISTRIBUTION:

I suggested that we should have a brief run through Charley's Order for Directions and see how it compared with my own documentation which we had considered earlier. We started with the appointment.

APPOINTMENTS—NOMINATED OR CONSENSUAL

Their appointments, like mine, came either from the parties, i.e. consensual appointments, or from an appointing body such as the RICS. Reflecting on their nominated appointments, Charley said that the first difference that came to mind was the significant number of early settlements which occurred following such appointments. On the other hand, the majority of their consensual appointments proceeded to an award, as in such cases the parties were clearly at issue and it would be unlikely they would settle their differences. With the majority of nominated appointments resulting in resolution of the dispute by the parties at an early stage, it seemed to him that parties often used the ploy of seeking a nomination as a tactic to test the strength of the opposing party's case and in the hope of precipitating a settlement.

Recognising this, it is common practice amongst rent review arbitrators to invite the joint agreement of the parties to a deferral of procedure for a short time to allow further negotiations in the hope that a settlement will result. They hold the view that it would not be in the interests of the arbitration generally to proceed immediately and thus impose significant costs on the parties which would be wasted if they were to settle shortly after. Charley has found that parties are generally reluctant to put their cards on the table and thus expose their weaknesses in the early stages of the dispute. I said that I suspected that this reluctance was not peculiar to rent review disputants.

ORAL HEARING OR "DOCUMENTS ONLY"?

Charley said that many of their cases which do proceed to an award are conducted without legal representatives on "documents only" with written representations and replies prepared by valuer experts.

Despite the clear advantages of an oral hearing in giving the opportunity to cross-examine the other side and ensure that the arbitrator thoroughly understands the issues, the parties and their non-legal representatives seem to have an in-built reluctance to request a hearing in rent review arbitrations.

Charley speculated that this might be due to a genuine fear of oral proceedings on the part of the advocate/expert; a feeling of inadequacy among his peers and an erroneous belief that charisma will rule the day—at least that is the impression that Charley and his pupil master have formed after a great number of such references.

I told Charley about a shooting pal of mine who runs a cattle market, who does a lot of arbitrations involving agricultural holdings, and there they invariably hold oral hearings. So it seems that not all rent review arbitrators share a genuine fear of oral hearings.

It seems from what Charley told us that problems frequently arise when a party's representative is taking on a dual role as advocate and expert. Many lack experience in advocacy and do not understand the difference between the two roles. Where this lack of understanding is apparent, their practice is to deal with it at the preliminary meeting. In a nutshell, they tell these representatives what they are entitled to expect to receive from the other side and what they have a duty to present by way of witness evidence and legal submissions. They also tell them how they are expected to conduct themselves at the hearing, if there is one—for example, how the representative, as advocate, deals with the re-examination of his own case. Charley said that since AA '96, preliminary meetings have become more prevalent.

The parties' representatives are eager to learn of the possible new procedures and the arbitrator's attitude to them. This is very helpful to the arbitrator, who can explain the new opportunities. These include the parties' opportunity to agree procedural and evidential matters and the arbitrator's residual discretion to adopt procedures for a fair resolution of the dispute without unnecessary delay or expense (s.1).

Despite the difficulties of an advocate/expert role many take this on, especially in smaller rent review disputes. Provided they remember which of the dual roles they are playing when addressing the arbitrator, many carry out the task entrusted to them very well. If only, Charley said, all advocate/experts would realise that any failure to distinguish their expert duties and their duties as the parties' representatives under section 40 contributed to the arbitrator's problems rather than advanced their party's case.

Charley told us that they had identified four distinct functions undertaken by rent review specialists—advising; negotiating; and acting as an advocate or as an expert witness. The duties of each were quite different. The important thing was for them to recognise which function they were fulfilling at any one time.

They have perceived that not all experts know that they are protected from liability for the evidence they give—perjury and negligence aside—and the work principally and proximately leading thereto. If they did, Charley felt that they might be more inclined to be more open with their clients. Any suggestion of "riding to orders", especially in a "documents only" procedure, would be negated if the expert presented the case recognising his responsibilities to the tribunal.

These responsibilities were set out in *National Justice Compania Naviera SA* v. *Prudential Assurance Company Ltd (The Ikarian Reefer)* (1993). In *London & Leeds Estate Limited* v. *Paribas Limited (No. 2)*, 28 July 1994, Mance J made the expert's position clear when he said:

"[the issue of truthfulness is fundamental and], in my judgment, [applies] with respect to the need to resist any subconscious tendency for an expert to become a member of a team and, as a result, to proffer views unduly favourable to the position of the party instructing him."

Charley said that in "documents only" procedures they had frequently to remind these experts of their duties, by pointing out that an arbitrator is not an independent expert and must not develop rival arguments or fill deficiencies in a party's case, as that would suggest partiality contrary to section 33. The essence of the difference between an arbitrator and an independent expert is that an arbitrator makes an award on the evidence adduced and the submissions on law. An independent expert is not fettered by the parties' representations and has a duty to investigate matters relevant to his determination with a standard of care tested against the body of professional opinion.

In any event, Charley now perceives a changing attitude, in that non-legal representatives of late appear more willing and eager to request a hearing and "have a go". It seems that they have realised that not only are there the advantages of cross-examination and face-to-face "understanding" with the arbitrator, but there can be significant costs savings. The issues have to be identified and are more readily narrowed where there is a hearing, whereas in a "documents only" procedure there is less pressure on the representatives to do this.

Written representations often widen and fudge the issues, leaving the arbitrator to sort out a mass of material in searching for the issues himself. In practice the "documents only" procedure does not generally encourage proper and appropriate witness evidence and development of legal submissions. In summary, Charley said that he feels that hearings discourage vagueness, whereas written representations encourage it. He hopes that with the opportunities in the new Act arbitrators will be persuaded to manage the arbitration more pro-actively, which will help to identify and narrow the issues.

Provided the arbitrator is managing the arbitration properly on the issues, witnesses, written openings and/or closings (if appropriate), a rent review hearing usually lasts no longer than three days, and often less, unless there are complex issues within the dispute requiring lengthy cross-examination or legal submissions.

Charley told us that his pupil master has toyed with the idea of preparing a paper on the subject of "How to Present a Case in a Rent Review Arbitration" and provide a précis of it to the parties early on in the reference. However, on reflection he thought this might not be a good idea because a question of partiality might arise, especially if one party clearly had an inferior level of representation to the other.

PLEADINGS OR STATEMENT OF CASE?

Following the appointment, the next difference between our respective procedures which occurred to Charley concerned the question of "pleadings".

In many cases formal pleadings are not appropriate as the parties clearly know what the dispute is. There is no cause of action as such, and the award will be a declaratory one on value, not the award of a sum of money.

While the Statement of Case is well understood by most rent review arbitrators, there are times when formal pleadings are appropriate and, in such cases or where both parties request them, such should be directed by the arbitrator.

The advantages and disadvantages of formal pleadings can be said to be as follows.

Advantages

(a) They identify the issues with some precision, including the legal basis of claim, allegations of default and consequential financial loss.
(b) They are easily susceptible to more detailed scrutiny and elaboration (requests for further and better particulars), particularly through formal rules of pleading, e.g. state basis of alleged knowledge, state positive case where omission or breach of duty is alleged, disclose documents expressly mentioned.
(c) The claimant is tied down to a specific case, but alternative claims can be accommodated.
(d) The standard presentation is well recognised by professionals, with guidance from *Supreme Court Practice* (the *White Book*).
(e) They distil the experience of professionals over more than a century.

Disadvantages

(a) The need for precision often leads to over-elaboration, and it is difficult to tell what is really in dispute.
(b) Lengthy requests for particulars are commonplace and the replies are not always illuminating (or necessary to the dispute).
(c) The issues on the pleadings often multiply alarmingly, making preparation of expert and factual evidence burdensome.
(d) The adoption of procedures is designed for court hearing and can lead to excessive formality and legalism.
(e) Formal pleadings need experience and skill (e.g. the distinction between material facts and evidence to prove those facts is often not understood) and often need extensive underlying knowledge of the law (e.g. as to implied terms or incorporation of express terms).

This then covers basic formal pleadings, but there are many other equally suitable ways of pleading a case. A simple exchange of letters (in a relatively straightforward factual one-off dispute), a Scott Schedule, a Statement of Case or a combination of any of those may well be appropriate in the circumstances of any particular reference.

The arbitrator should approach every reference with an entirely open mind. He has a duty under section 33 AA '96 to:

"adopt procedures suitable to the circumstances of the particular case"

as well as

"avoiding unnecessary expense and delay",

although the arbitrator is further bound to

"comply with that general duty in conducting the arbitral proceedings, in its decisions on matters of procedure and evidence",

which I take to be a clear reference to the manner in which the arbitrator directs each party to state its case. His freedom to dictate the form of such statements depends upon what, if anything, the parties have agreed under section 34 AA '96.

Differences between Statements of Case and Formal Pleadings

The difference between Statements of Case and Formal Pleadings can be summarised as follows:

(a) Statements of Case and Defence set out not only material facts alleged but argument in support of the case and, to some extent, the evidence to be given in support.

(b) In construction cases the evidence is contained in documents, including the contractual documentation; site or progress minutes; drawings; variation orders and correspondence, copies of which form annexures to the narrative statements of case or defence.

(c) What is put before the opposing party and the arbitrator is more selective, each party seeking to concentrate upon those matters and documents which most support its case. This can result in a different approach to the adversarial one of pleading concisely and attacking the opponent's pleading.

The statement of case approach is often desired by claimants particularly if, e.g. in a claim for delay and extras, a claim document has been prepared and submitted to the employer before arbitration has become necessary; conversely, a reluctant respondent may well prefer the service of more formal pleadings, especially where it is thought that the claimant's case appears strong on paper.

Advantages of the Statement of Case procedure over Formal Pleadings

The advantages of the Statement of Case procedure over Formal Pleadings could be said to be as follows:

(a) A Statement of Case (or Defence) will refer to the significant points of fact, evidence, law and argument which the client regards as important and should concentrate on the main issues rather than introduce peripheral matters.

(b) The procedure is likely to lead to an earlier hearing or to a determination without the need for a formal hearing at all.

(c) Both parties will want to put their best case forward and not hold back ammunition for a tactical ambush later in the arbitration.

(d) A more positive and inquisitorial role is given to the arbitrator (although the arbitrator can acquire this power by default if the parties do not agree otherwise by virtue of section 34 AA '96).

(e) A Statement of Case can be written by a layperson without the intervention of lawyers.

Disadvantages of the Statement of Case procedure

(a) The points identified by the parties will not always be the most significant.

(b) The combination of evidence, law and argument in the Statement of Case may lead to bad points being taken, e.g. arguments on points of law which do not arise on the facts, evidential disputes which cannot affect legal positions.

(c) Either party may attempt to shift ground late in the arbitration on the basis that their new case is subsumed in their general submission.

(d) The requirement to disclose evidence is burdensome if done properly and potentially misleading if done superficially.
(e) The arbitrator has fewer guidelines to assist him as to the scope of the dispute and its means of resolution and the possibility of misconduct in procedure increases.

Having explained this to Thomasina, I then pointed out to her some of the things to look out for in pleadings, whether Formal or Statement of Case.

Defences

On Defences, as respondents do not bear the burden of proof, many points of Defence consist of little more than denials, and are often uninformative:

"An artfully drawn defence may conceal as much as it reveals."

Often respondents refuse to admit the obvious; they should be required to:

(a) Specify more precisely what issues they dispute, how far they are disputed, and on what basis they are disputed.
(b) Show their hand evidentially.
(c) Disclose any defence of law upon which they rely.

When to use Formal Pleading or a Statement of Case is a matter for discussion between the parties and the arbitrator.

Unless the parties are represented by counsel I suggest opting for the Statement of Case every time—it does not require so much expertise to draft and should ensure a speedy resolution.

As in other arbitral disciplines, it would be a serious irregularity (s.68) to refuse to abide by the parties' joint procedural request (s.34). The arbitrator cannot override the parties' agreed procedure; all the arbitrator can do, in such circumstances, if he is not prepared to accede to their joint request, is to resign (s.25). Not a course of action of which I approve, I told Charley.

Thomasina chipped in at this stage and reminded me that I had always told her that an arbitrator could not retire and could only refuse to act. I agreed that that was my view prior to AA '96. Now, an arbitrator clearly has a right to resign, but I would deal with this later (see p.173).

THE ARBITRATOR'S DUTY IN RENT REVIEW DISPUTES

Charley said that in some circles it had been suggested that an arbitrator's overriding duty in a rent review dispute is to arrive at the correct rent. His pupil master does not accept this. He maintains that it runs contrary to the principle of arbitration to determine the dispute (and the rent) solely from the evidence adduced.

As in any other arbitration, the rent review arbitrator must disclose any material facts of which he is aware which he would be unable to put out of his mind, and thus invite comment on such facts by the parties. If, as some practitioners suggest, he proceeded on the basis of arriving at the correct rent he would be acting as an independent expert which, of course, he must not do. Charley says that he can think of three occasions when he would be minded to introduce new material:

(i) when he was aware of a helpful comparable rent which went to the root of the issue and he could not put it out of his mind;
(ii) when the band of contentions was clearly far removed from the band of sustainable rental value;
(iii) when submissions of law did not accord with settled legal principles.

THE PROCESS OF REASONING IN RENT REVIEW CASES

On how the rent review arbitrator should approach the process of reasoning, Charley referred us to the judgment in *Vinava Shipping Co. Ltd v. Finelvet AG (The Chrysalis)* (1982). While this is a shipping case, the process of reasoning is relevant to rent review arbitrators. In this case, after identifying the first two stages (as to law and fact) Mustill J said:

"(3) In the light of the facts and the law so ascertained, the arbitrator reaches his decision.

In some cases, the third stage will be purely mechanical. Once the law is correctly ascertained, the decision follows inevitably from the application of it to the facts found. In other instances, however, the third stage involves an element of judgement on the part of the arbitrator. There is no uniquely 'right' answer to be derived from marrying the facts and the law, merely a choice of answers, none of which can be described as wrong."

Thomasina suggested, quite brightly I thought, that it must surely be right that the "element of judgement" is a value judgement on the evidence adduced.

Many rent review cases do not involve issues of law; they are confined to issues of fact. The arbitrator is left to weigh the conflicting opinion evidence of expert witnesses, sometimes without truly comparable transactions, applying the "element of judgement" referred to in *The Chrysalis*. Charley suggested that this is probably why the parties could not settle in the first place. It becomes all the more important that experts should recognise their responsibilities and the extent of the evidence they may present. Formal qualifications in such circumstances can be of secondary importance to knowledge and experience of the market in the relevant property. It is not unknown for there to be no truly comparable transactions available, and thus the arbitrator is left to decide between the conflicting opinion evidence. He then has to rely on the knowledge and experience of the expert witnesses, using his value judgement, to decide the rent on the evidence given. (See also *Ravenseft Properties Ltd* v. *Boots Properties Ltd*, QBD, 24 March 1997.)

PROCEDURAL PROBLEMS IN RENT REVIEW ARBITRATIONS

Procedural problems, as in other types of arbitration, are generally alleviated by the arbitrator proactively managing the arbitration. The most common problems in rent review arbitrations are:

(a) constructional issues on the wording of the rent review clause;
(b) the admissibility of evidence;
(c) evaluating opinion evidence.

Charley then dealt with each of these in turn.

Constructional issues

Such issues, he said, have over the years tended to vary. However, they mainly occur, he suggested, when significant forensic legal input is required, because of the large amounts of money at stake where the annual rent awarded is likely to be fixed for five years. Charley said he felt that new issues will continue to be identified, and there will be no reduction in the extent to which those issues will be litigated.

Over the years such issues have included distinguishing between the literal and commercial commonsense approaches; the disregard of improvements; the notional term with, or without, rent reviews; the effect of user and alienation restrictions; fixtures and fittings and treatment of rent-free periods for fitting out and inducements. An experienced rent review specialist will have no difficulty in identifying with these issues; the solutions are another matter!

Admissibility of evidence

AA '96 (s.34(2)(f)) and the Civil Evidence Act 1995 (CEA '95) have provided much-needed help in rent review arbitrations. Prior to these enactments, interlocutory issues on admissibility of evidence were frequent. Now, hearsay evidence is admissible, with the weight to be attached to it left in the arbitrator's hands. If the parties jointly agreed, or the arbitrator with his residual discretion decided, that the strict rules should apply, CEA '95 would allow either party, after compliance with the notice requirements in the Act, to introduce hearsay evidence. For this reason Charley said that most rent review arbitrators are unlikely to apply the strict rules of evidence (unless that evidence truly went to the root of the issue and was disputed), leaving the parties to produce their evidence in the forms they preferred. However, the arbitrator would be entitled to take account of the quality of the evidence in the weight he attached to it. It is up to the parties to produce the evidence and its quality is in their hands also.

In "documents only" procedures the strict rules of evidence cannot apply. Experts often introduce evidence of transactions not within their personal knowledge, usually supported by written confirmation of the details of the transaction from the person who dealt with it. It is implied that if the parties have requested a written representations procedure and the arbitrator has agreed (of course, reserving to himself the right to call the hearing should he so decide), a written statement of facts by someone other than the expert representing the party would, in itself, be a written representation and, therefore, admissible. This is yet another incidence where the disadvantage of a "documents only" procedure is highlighted; the opposing party will not have the opportunity to cross-examine the maker of the written statement of fact.

It is clear that the parties, their representatives and the arbitrator may all be misled by such statements as none of them know the surrounding circumstances and the evidence cannot be tested under cross-examination, especially if the source of the transaction as evidence is from one side only.

Charley referred us to several cases dealing with the admissibility of trading accounts particularly relevant in rents for licensed and leisure properties. Despite criticism, the law currently stands that the actual tenant's trading accounts are inadmissible (unless they are in the public domain or are introduced as evidence of earning capacity for specialised property when the market would be likely to disclose such accounts), because they are not a relevant matter having probative value. I reminded Thomasina that I had touched on this subject on a previous occasion when we had a discussion on the admissibility of evidence (see p.71).

Previous rent review awards in commercial property cases are apparently inadmissible because they are not sufficiently relevant to the market rent which is the subject of the dispute. But, Charley said, rent review arbitrators should never overlook the fact that, if no objection has been raised to the admissibility of the evidence of a transaction, thereby attracting implied waiver, it would probably amount to misconduct (or, as it is now called, *serious irregularity*, I reminded Charley) for the arbitrator not to consider that evidence as material.

I pointed out to Charley that, in agricultural cases, there is a statutory requirement that an arbitrator shall take other awards into account (see Schedule 2, paragraph (1)(3) Agricultural Holdings Act 1986, which says "... the Arbitrator shall take into account" evidence of rents including those fixed by arbitration under the Act). The agricultural rent review boys take the view that it goes without saying that the only way of doing so is to have the awards (in other arbitrations) before the arbitrator. Such awards are required to contain reasons by virtue of Schedule 11, paragraph 21 of the Agricultural Holdings Act 1986, so they contain a full explanation of how the rent was arrived at because of the very specific matters to be dealt with by virtue of Schedule 2.

Hold on, Godfather, interjected Thomasina, this is all getting a bit heavy for me. I don't really want to know about the niceties of agricultural arbitration at this stage. These schedules you mention and this Agricultural Act mean nothing to me. Sorry, I said, you are absolutely right. I got carried away. Right, back to basics, Charley. What next? Opinion evidence, I think, said Charley.

Evaluating opinion evidence

The third area where rent review arbitrators appear to encounter problems is over conflicting expert evidence—where opposing parties adopt different methods of valuation, neither recognising the other party's method as valid.

Charley said that it can be argued that, in this instance, the arbitrator must find wholly for one party or the other; the evidence does not admit to a figure between the two contentions. Charley's pupil master holds the view that, in such circumstances, the arbitrator should invite the expert whose valuation he is inclined to reject to comment on the other expert's figure in the valuation method which he prefers. Of course, it could be that the arbitrator does not favour either method, i.e. he does not agree with either expert.

Charley told us how it seems a peculiar trait of rent review experts that they rarely alter the figure for which they are contending; this is apparently especially prevalent in "documents only" procedures. One would have hoped that there would be many occasions when an expert would, in recognising his responsibility to assist the tribunal, amend his figure having considered the other side's statement of case, but apparently this rarely occurs; the experts, almost invariably, stick rigidly to their original figures.

If the arbitrator did disagree with both experts, Charley agreed that it was important for him to inform them both, keeping the lessons of *Fox* v. *Wellfair* in mind—i.e. telling them what was in his mind and allowing them to address him on it, similar to using his own expertise (see p.172). (See also *Ravenseft Properties Ltd* v. *Boots Properties Ltd*, QBD, 24 March 1997.)

Thomasina pointed out that a number of reported cases in this context revealed a prevalent failure among rent review arbitrators to abide by these principles. The main stumbling blocks seem to occur over the role of the rent review arbitrator itself. Clearly some find difficulty in changing from independent expert to arbitrator.

It is the case that many aspiring, and indeed practising, arbitrators accept appointments as independent experts making rent review determinations. As Charley pointed out, as independent experts they, of course, have a duty to investigate the issues. However, when acting as arbitrators they must resist the temptation; they must adapt to the strict discipline of using their general knowledge and experience to understand the evidence and not rely on secret evidence. The distinction is clearly set out in *Fox* v. *Wellfair*. Charley said that section 34(2)(g) does not alter the requirement for an arbitrator to introduce any secret evidence on which he intends to rely for comment by the parties (see p.172).

Once again we reminded ourselves that arbitrators are not appointed to investigate the truth of the matter, but to decide the issue in favour of the party who has convinced him on the balance of probabilities.

Rent review arbitrators, however, face an added practical difficulty, especially in "documents only" procedures, if the issues are not clearly identified and/or the rival arguments have not been developed adequately—hence the argument for a hearing.

REASONS IN RENT REVIEW DISPUTE AWARDS

Guidance from the courts on the content and extent of reasons is, of course, no different in rent review arbitrations. Sir Thomas Bingham's address to the Chartered Institute of Arbitrators in 1987, entitled "Differences between a Judgment and a Reasoned Award", continues to stand as an exemplary paper on the subject and, Charley believes, should be read by all arbitrators when embarking on their earliest awards. This was a sentiment with which I could not disagree.

On the question of reasons, Charley said that many rent review arbitrations, especially the smaller ones, rest solely on issues of fact, requiring a value judgement on conflicting opinion evidence on the analysis of comparable factual evidence; and occasionally conflicting opinion evidence without factual evidence of comparable transactions.

Charley's pupil master considers that it must be good practice, in any event, to ascertain from the parties the extent of any reasons sought. For example, if a party merely wants to know how the arbitrator did his arithmetic, including the amount of the rent per square foot and any end-user allowances, this does not require reference to, and findings on, all material comparable transactions to be adduced—instead of being several pages in length, the reasons need to be no more than a few lines. It reflects the principles of avoiding unnecessary delay or expense (s.1 and s.33).

On the other hand the parties or a party may require findings on all matters upon which a party places significant reliance. Reasons under AA '96, he said, require such findings in sufficient detail for the court to consider any question of law arising therefrom; and the question whether there is any evidence to support a finding of fact is accepted as being a question of law.

Charley then reminded us that rent review arbitrators sometimes publish an award in the alternative, where there is a clearly identified issue of law which each party interprets differently. Of course, the arbitrator has to decide this issue of law, as not to do so would leave the award unenforceable and lacking the substantive requirements of certainty and finality. Having made his holding on the issue of law, the arbitrator then finds the amount of the rent consequent upon that determination.

However, he includes in his award the amount of the rent he would have determined if he had decided the issue of law in the alternative. In the event of the issue of law then being referred to the court, the result of the court's decision on that issue of law would automatically determine which of the two alternative rental figures applied without the necessity of remitting the award to the arbitrator for further consideration.

That ended our discussion on the differences between our two arbitral disciplines, which we had both found interesting, if a little strange in parts. Having said that, apart from the odd quaint practice, most of what Charley had told us matched our own understanding of proper arbitral practice. As a parting shot Charley said he would be happy to show us a typical simple rent review award (sanitised, of course, by removing the names of the parties).

Although delighted at the prospect, it was late and I really thought that we had had enough for one day. I accepted his kind offer but said that we would defer it until we came to consider awards ourselves (see p.196 for Charley's award).

Instead, I said, why don't we adjourn to the local hostelry for a glass or two of bubbly—I think we all deserve it!

CHAPTER 7

WHAT IS THIS INTERLOCUTORY PERIOD?

GENERAL

What is this interlocutory period and these interlocutory directions that we hear about? asked Thomasina.

Quite simply, I said, it is the period between the commencement of the arbitration, in our case the preliminary meeting (although strictly even that is part of the interlocutory process), and the conclusion of the reference; in our case, the hearing.

In effect, I said, it is the period during which the arbitrator ensures the smooth running of the reference. I suggested that Thomasina look through our Orders for Directions to identify matters with which the arbitrator was likely to have to deal before the hearing. For example, the first thing that is going to happen is that the arbitrator will receive the parties' Statements. These in themselves will generate some correspondence. It may be that one party will complain of the other's Statement: that it is not properly particularised or does not comply with the arbitrator's directions, in as much as it does not include either principal documents or a list of those such documents.

It may be that one of the parties will apply to the arbitrator for an order to restrain the other party from doing something.

There may be an application for specific discovery or for further and better particulars of one of the parties' Statements or Reply and so on. There are many matters on which the arbitrator is likely to be informed during this interlocutory process.

Although I discourage the parties from sending me copies of all correspondence between their representatives, in some references parties use the arbitrator as a means of coercing co-operation out of the other party. By copying the arbitrator in to correspondence containing requests that party hopes that the other party will be intimidated into compliance.

What the arbitrator should remember, at all times during this period, is his duty "... to avoid unnecessary delay and expense..." (s.33 AA '96): this in the face, perhaps, of a reluctant respondent who may not be interested in a speedy resolution of the dispute. Indeed, it could well suit his book to delay matters as long as possible. As long as he is in funds that he does not have to pay to the claimant, despite his mounting legal costs, he will be content to disrupt the proceedings. This arbitrator's duty to avoid unnecessary delay must be balanced against a party's desire to present the fullest case that he can.

As long as the arbitrator recognises the rules of natural justice, which we looked at earlier, I said, he would not go far wrong; that is, to give each party the opportunity of presenting its case and answering the case made against it. Be even-handed, particularly when you are attempting to limit costs by curtailing the procedure. Never communicate with one party in the absence of the other.

WHAT SORT OF INTERLOCUTORY DIRECTIONS?

When Thomasina asked what sort of interlocutory directions, I said that we have already mentioned one or two of the most common—applications for further and better particulars; applications for specific discovery; applications for security for costs and so on. The best way that I could illustrate these was to show her an example. The one I chose incorporated a number of directions in normal correspondence. I explained that I have taken to giving directions in letter form in quite a number of instances—I think it more user-friendly.

However, I then add something to the effect of "for the avoidance of doubt this letter can be taken as my Order for Directions No..." so as to dispel any doubt whether or not it is a proper direction. We then looked at my example, which is an extract from a letter covering a number of applications.

SCOTT SCHEDULE

I note what the parties say about this issue and I find the Respondent's submission has some merit. I can understand that their hands are tied without the Claimant's tender build-up. However, having said that, the Respondent could have made more effort to have obtained the necessary information and, in that respect, the Claimant's approach is not unreasonable but it could perhaps have been brought to my attention earlier.

> ACCORDINGLY, I HEREBY DIRECT that the Claimant gives specific discovery to the Respondent not later than 5.00 p.m. 25 February 1999, of the "build-up" of its tender on which the sum quoted in Order 08/3069/2938, 2 July 1997, was based.
>
> The Respondent to revise its comments on the Scott Schedule, in particular in respect of quantum. This Amended Scott Schedule to be served upon the Claimant, and copied to me, not later than 14 days after receipt of the Claimant's tender "build-up".
>
> Neither party will be permitted to present any case in respect of each of the variations other than that which is pleaded in its comments section of the Scott Schedule; and
>
> Neither party will be permitted to adduce any positive evidence as to quantum, different to those figures pleaded, in relation to each of the variations claimed in the Scott Schedule as to quantum, subject to liability.
>
> Liberty to apply.

REQUESTS FOR FURTHER AND BETTER PARTICULARS

Both parties have served Draft Requests. I asked Jayrich Associates, in my letter 18 February, whether or not they were prepared to respond voluntarily to the Respondent's Draft Request for Further and Better Particulars of the Statement of Case, but I do not see a specific answer to this. However, both parties seem to appreciate the importance of co-operation and I have already set out, in my Second Letter 20 February, the process into which we will be forced if either party refuses to answer the other party's Requests. I am therefore assuming that each party will Reply voluntarily to the other party's Draft Request, but I ask each party to scrutinise their Draft and withdraw any Request which they consider might cause difficulties, or which they can manage without.

> ACCORDINGLY I DIRECT THAT both parties, having agreed to voluntarily Reply to the other party's Request for Further and Better Particulars of that party's case, do so not later than 5.00 p.m. 13 March 1999.
>
> If either party objects to any particular Request to the point where they refuse to Reply, or simply cannot Reply, then they are to inform the other party, with their reasons, not later than 5.00 p.m. 28 February 1999 to give that party the opportunity of withdrawing that Request.
>
> Not later than 5.00 p.m. 6 March 1999 I am to be informed if there are any outstanding unanswered Requests which either party consider a Reply is essential in order to understand the case it has to answer. In which case, after considering these unanswered Requests, and the other party's reasons for not answering them, I will issue a separate Direction for an oral hearing to resolve the matter.
>
> Liberty to Apply.

Although I agreed that we had touched on some of these issues when we went through the preliminary meeting agenda, I suggested that we looked at two of these directions in a little more detail.

Further and better particulars (see pp.39 and 65)

So as to alert the parties to the tests which I would apply in deciding whether or not to grant any such request, I set out this criterion in my agenda for the preliminary meeting (see item 10.03.2.7, p.39).

I pointed out to Thomasina that while making it clear to the parties that I discourage applications for further and better particulars—the Statements of Case should be properly and adequately pleaded in the first place—in complex cases, involving many thousands of documents, it is almost inevitable that some further particularisation will reasonably be required.

As an alternative to considering Requests for further and better particulars, the arbitrator has the choice of saying that he does not accept the statement to which the request applies; it has not been properly served and notice given to the claimant; unless it is properly particularised within seven days he will proceed as if that party is not going to serve that statement. This is a draconian measure which I believe should only be used in extreme cases. Far better to allow the opposing party to raise a "Request" for further and better particulars.

It must be remembered that a common way of attacking your opponent's pleading is to apply for particulars. It is not uncommon for an application to be made to strike out or for amendment:

(a) where there was no reasonable cause of action or defence disclosed;
(b) where claim or defence is frivolous, vexatious or an abuse;
(c) where objectionable matters are included.

I reminded Thomasina that the object of particulars is to enable the party seeking them to know the case he has to meet at the hearing and to avoid being taken by surprise. Apart from that sensible objective, if achieved by a request for particulars, other advantages are:

(a) Establishing what the opponent is relying upon: oral evidence or documents, to prove a material fact alleged.

(b) Limitation of an issue: the opponent is bound by the particulars and cannot at the hearing (usually) go into any matters not fairly included in them.

It was thought that particulars tended to narrow the issues, and therefore should be encouraged. So much for the theory. I should have thought that modern pleadings achieved these objectives, I said.

I recalled a solicitor, speaking at a seminar on pleadings, saying that in practice Requests for particulars are often used, not to ascertain the case which the party serving the request is to meet at the hearing, but to put the party providing the particulars to trouble, delay and expense, with the object of slowing down the proceedings or making that party less inclined to pursue its case, or both.

He gave the following as an example:

> C produces claim document to R for delay, additional works, variations and disruption. Claim rejected in entirety even though R (the main contractor) resolves its own claim with employer. C, the subcontractor, refers claim to arbitration, but encounters delaying tactics over proper jurisdiction; appointment of arbitrator; alleged conflict of interest by counsel and solicitors acting for C—all of which occurs in Commercial Court. Arbitration proceeds. Points of claim served. R waits 12 months, the time allowed to serve Points of Defence, then contends that it cannot formulate such points until after particulars of claim are provided in answer to a very lengthy requests for particulars sought of each paragraph of the Points of Claim.

Can it reasonably be said that R does not know the case it has to resist?

He then asked us: what should the arbitrator have done in these circumstances?

I remember asking at the time what sort of arbitrator would allow 12 months to serve the points of defence? (Particularly bearing in mind the duty imposed upon the arbitrator under section 33 AA '96 to avoid unnecessary delay.) I think that the longest I have ever allowed in the most complex of cases was 56 days. The arbitrator must have been aware of the respondent's delaying tactics over the period following reference to arbitration, his appointment and subsequent challenge to his jurisdiction, etc. If it was clear to him that some of this was a pure delaying tactic and prima facie unjustified then he should bear that conduct in mind when responding to the respondent's Request for further and better particulars.

The arbitrator would still have to ask himself whether there was any substance in the respondent's request, applying his own test to the questions asked.

If he decided to order the claimant to answer all or some of the respondent's Requests, which he, the arbitrator, detailed, then he should apply a tight timetable to both the Reply to the Request and the subsequent service of any statement delayed by that Request.

Disadvantages

The disadvantages of further and better particulars may be said to be as follows:
- (a) by serving a Request for particulars the requesting party may alert the opposing party to a defect in its pleaded case and enable it to avoid what could be a serious flaw in that case;
- (b) if seeking to proceed quickly, a party may be better advised not to clog up the works with a Request for particulars, unless the pleaded case against it is so obscure that it would be dangerous not to serve a Request;
- (c) seeking particulars invariably adds to the costs of the proceedings, often with little to show for it.

If a pleading is subjected to a lengthy or difficult Request for particulars which proved problematic, that pleading and the case have not been properly prepared: there should not be requests for particulars. When preparing a pleading, after it is drafted any solicitor or barrister worth his salt should play "devil's advocate" and pretend to be acting for the opposing party. If it is possible to prepare a request for particulars the job has not been done well.

If faced with a badly pleaded case, it is sometimes tactically sound not to seek further and better particulars, especially if there is a wish to make speedy progress in the arbitration. Even if considered desirable for tactical or strategic purposes, a Request for particulars may have adverse consequences, as highlighted.

Remember, I said, the old saying that I had mentioned before, that further and better particulars rarely live up to their name and never reveal "the Crown Jewels".

Failure to comply with direction for further and better particulars

What if one party failed to comply with my directions concerning pleadings or a direction to provide further and better particulars? Thomasina asked.

I told her that one solution is to resort to an Unless Order. This order will set a reasonable time limit for compliance, failing which the arbitrator may reserve the right to consider striking out that part of the claim to which the particulars relate.

Should the further and better particulars relate to the entirety of the claimant's claim, the arbitrator's Unless Order would have to be followed by a Peremptory Order on the same lines as the Unless Order, threatening to strike out the claimant's claim (s.41(5)) on the lines of that set out below.

Unless Order in respect of failure to reply to further and better particulars

IN THE MATTER OF THE ARBITRATION ACT 1996

AND

IN THE MATTER OF AN ARBITRATION UNDER THE JCT 1998 EDITION OF THE CONSTRUCTION INDUSTRY MODEL ARBITRATION RULES

BETWEEN

RELIABLE BUILDERS LTD   Claimant

SANCTUARY HOUSE LTD   Respondent

ORDER FOR DIRECTIONS NO 18—UNLESS ORDER

Re Further and Better Particulars

WHEREAS

1.00 The Claimant, by letter 15 November 1998, requested the Respondent to clarify some points of the Statement of Defence and Counterclaim served on 18 October 1998. The Respondent informed me that he considered this to be a "fishing expedition" and did not intend to reply.

2.00 The Claimant has now requested me to order the Respondent to provide further and better particulars of this Statement of Defence and Counterclaim and

3.00 I have considered the Request in the light of the criteria which I outlined at the Preliminary Meeting with the parties, 23 March 1998, and agree that the particulars sought meet this criteria.

ACCORDINGLY I HEREBY DIRECT THAT

4.00 That the Respondent serve a Reply to these Further and Better Particulars not later than 5.00 p.m. on 1 November 1998.

5.00 Should the Respondent fail to provide fully particularised

148 What is this interlocutory period?

answers to this Request he will be debarred from counterclaiming those items not properly particularised.

6.00 Liberty to Apply.

7.00 Costs of the Claimant's application in connection with this Order and the costs of this Order to be paid by the Respondent in any event.

Date: 15 November 1998

D. Mark Cato MSc FRICS FCIArb
Registered Arbitrator

To: Jayrich Associates   Representatives of the Claimant
                                        FAO Joel Redman

To: Kalmsyde & Joyoff   Solicitors for the Respondent
                                        FAO James Crighton

What sort of interlocutory directions? 149

If the default continued, I said, the arbitrator could consent to an application by the respondent to the court under section 42(1) AA '96, requiring the claimant to comply with the Peremptory Order. Then if the claimant still failed to comply and there was a counterclaim, the reference would continue to determine that counterclaim.

Alternatives to further and better particulars

Notices to Admit Facts and Interrogatories

Apart from further and better particulars, I told Thomasina that there were two other cost-effective devices for narrowing the issues—Notices to Admit Facts and Interrogatories.

The Notice to Admit Facts is usually made by one party to the other inviting him to agree that his assertions are true. Once made, these facts are binding on the party making the admission. If, however, the party to whom the request is made fails or refuses to agree and the asking party is put to proof of these assertions which are subsequently proved to be true then, depending upon the circumstances, the arbitrator will be at liberty to take this conduct into account when dealing with costs. Here again, such notices should not be necessary in arbitration, but occasionally one does come up against a reluctant respondent who, although he participates in the reference, does so with bad grace and therefore needs chivvying along from time to time.

She might recall item 17.00 from my direction following the preliminary meeting:

> "Common ground
> Correspondence, plans, photographs and figures shall be agreed as far as possible and a statement of this common ground shall be included in the agreed hearing bundle."

In a recent reference, I told Thomasina, towards the end of the period agreed for the exchange of statements, the claimant wrote to me complaining that he was having difficulty in gaining co-operation from the respondent in preparing this statement of common ground. This being so, the claimant asked if I would be prepared to order a Notice to Admit Facts.

150 What is this interlocutory period?

My initial response, as in all cases of alleged non-co-operation between the parties, was to write and encourage the defaulting party to toe the line voluntarily. An arbitrator should certainly not rush in issuing directions without giving the party against whom the complaint is being made the opportunity of putting his side of things, I said. It may well be that there is more to this alleged non-co-operation than the claimant has disclosed.

Having ascertained that what the claimant had averred reflected the true state of affairs, I reminded the respondent in this case of my direction and firmly requested him to comply without the need for a further direction which, in this case, would probably be a Notice to Admit Facts. I made it clear that if I was forced to issue further directions in order to obtain compliance with my earlier direction then I would not hesitate to order that any costs incidental to and arising from such direction would be paid by him.

This warning is more often than not sufficient to elicit co-operation, I told Thomasina. If not, then the arbitrator should have no compunction in agreeing to the claimant's request to issue a Notice to Admit Facts, as follows:

Typical Order re Notice to Admit Facts

IN THE MATTER OF THE ARBITRATION ACT 1996

AND

IN THE MATTER OF AN ARBITRATION UNDER THE JCT 1998 EDITION OF THE CONSTRUCTION INDUSTRY MODEL ARBITRATION RULES

BETWEEN

RELIABLE BUILDERS LTD   Claimant

SANCTUARY HOUSE LTD   Respondent

ORDER FOR DIRECTIONS NO 18

Re Notice to admit Facts

WHEREAS

1.00 The Claimant has requested the Respondent, by letter dated 13 December 1998, to admit the facts set out in that letter

and

WHEREAS

2.00 The Respondent has refused to admit the facts and the Claimant has requested me to allow him to serve a Notice to Admit Facts on the Respondent

I HEREBY DIRECT THAT

3.00 The Claimant serve such Notice forthwith and that the Respondent shall Reply not later than 5.00 p.m. 20 December 1998

4.00 The costs of proving any facts listed in the Claimant's letter which, for no good reason, are not admitted by the Respondent's in his Reply, shall be paid by the Respondent.

5.00 The costs of the Claimant's application in connection with this Order and the costs of this Order to be paid by the Respondent in any event.

152 What is this interlocutory period?

Date: 13 November 1998.

D Mark Cato MSc FRICS FCIArb
Registered Arbitrator

To: Jayrich Associates   Representatives of the Claimant
FAO Joel Redman

To: Kalmsyde & Joyoff   Solicitors for the Respondent
FAO James Crighton

Was it really necessary, to use such formal language in your directions as WHEREAS and I HEREBY DIRECT THAT? Thomasina asked. Absolutely not, I said, it's purely a matter of personal choice. I have found that formal directions such as these are more likely to be complied with than more loosely worded informal directions. Every arbitrator develops his own style of directions, one style being no more correct than another. The important thing is that the direction should be clear and unambiguous.

We had pretty well exhausted the subject of Notices to Admit Facts, except to say that to ignore this device may be to lose an opportunity to narrow issues and to save the parties costs, which objective should always be at the forefront of the arbitrator's mind.

We then considered Interrogatories. I explained that when a pleading is not properly particularised, and this is clear to the arbitrator when he reviews it, an alternative to his ordering further and better particulars, which would usually follow a Request from the party on whom the pleading was served, is the administration of Interrogatories, *viz*. written questions addressed by one party to the other intended to be answered on oath.

This is a device used in the High Court (Order 26 RSC) but can be equally effective in arbitration.

It appears that before the AA '96 the arbitrator had power to order the administration of Interrogatories, but he could not unilaterally raise an Interrogatory; he could only do so in response to a Request from one of the parties. The problem with using Interrogatories is that it is considered by some to be a "formal and inflexible device".

However, AA '96 gives the arbitrator not only the power to order interrogatories (s.34(2)(e)), but also to submit written questions of his own.

For example this subsection provides, *inter alia*:

"whether and if so what questions should be put to and answered by the respective parties and when and in what form this should be done".

I would like to see much more use being made of asking written questions. Whether they are called Interrogatories or Notices to Admit Facts matters not—it is the prospective cost efficiency of this form of procedure which makes it so attractive (see Adversarial Or Inquisitorial Process?, p.169).

There was some interesting commentary on this power to order

154 What is this interlocutory period?

Interrogatories in two of the books published on the AA '96 shortly after it was enacted.

Harris, Planterose and Tecks had this to say of section 34(2)(e):

"This subsection gives a broad power to decide how, if at all, the parties should be questioned. It would, thus, include the use of interrogatories as found in the English court procedures, but since that method of proceeding is rarely truly suitable in court, it is even less likely to be so in arbitration. The provision is likely to have more relevance to arbitrations involving individuals rather than those involving corporate bodies.

It should obviously be read in conjunction with the following three subsections, which are all, to some extent, concerned with evidence and ascertaining the facts."

I told Thomasina that I respectfully disagreed with the learned authors concerning the extent to which the arbitrator asks questions. I believe the more inquisitorial approach now clearly available to arbitrators could prove to be one of the catalysts for the renaissance of arbitration.

This view seems to be shared, at least to some degree, by the authors of another book, Rutherford and Sims, who say this of the arbitrator asking questions:

"in a technical dispute where the parties are not legally represented, an arbitrator might dispense with a preliminary hearing, gathering all the relevant information he requires at that stage by sending the parties a list of questions to which he requires answers. This power can also be useful if the arbitrator, in an attempt to clarify certain issues, puts written questions to the parties to which he requires specific answers. Once knowing the general area of the dispute he might frame specific questions to the parties, the answers to which might narrow the issues, or assist the parties in drafting of their statements of case and defence.

To try to limit the issues in contention by seeking specific information from the parties in the way described above can be an efficient and effective way of managing the resolution of the dispute."

While the new thinking in connection with arbitrations and the more "hands on" approach open to arbitrators seem to be going towards the use of "Interrogatories", I said—if one can use that term to describe the process of the parties' questions—the courts' philosophy is to discourage such applications. The reason usually given for the courts' attitude over Interrogatories and Notices to Admit Facts is that Requests for particulars or further discovery of specific categories of documentation will, in most cases, prove to be an effective means of obtaining the required information.

Applications for Interrogatories, if made by the parties, should probably not be made until after close of pleadings and inspection of documents, or even possibly as late as after the exchange of witness statements and then, if one listens to the courts' arguments, only if there is no other convenient and effective course. The reason for delaying such Requests is that the required answers may well be provided in some documentation or other during this process. Questions put by the arbitrator may well fall into a different category and therefore could safely be asked earlier, for the reasons given above.

In summary, I said to Thomasina, while accepting the desirability of moving the arbitral process as far away as possible from High Court procedures, it must not be lost sight of that lawyers will continue to be involved in this process—and in certain circumstances, why shy away from using terminology that is familiar and well understood by the participants? With arbitrators being encouraged to take a more "hands on" or proactive role in the process, I can see that such devices could assist in this. Provided the parties have not made a contrary agreement, it is for the arbitrator to decide how he will obtain the evidence that he needs to determine the issues in dispute.

Finally, before we left the subject, we looked at a typical Request for Interrogatories.

156 What is this interlocutory period?

Typical Request for Interrogatories (questions from the arbitrator)

IN THE MATTER OF THE ARBITRATION ACT 1996

AND

IN THE MATTER OF AN ARBITRATION UNDER THE JCT 1998 EDITION OF THE CONSTRUCTION INDUSTRY MODEL ARBITRATION RULES

BETWEEN

RELIABLE BUILDERS   Claimant

SANCTUARY HOUSE LTD   Respondent

ORDER FOR DIRECTIONS NO 18

Re Interrogatories

Interrogatories on behalf of the above-named Claimant further to the Claimant's application dated 18 November 1998 and the arbitrator's consent being given by his letter 22 November 1998.

1. Do you accept that you received the letter of 22 August 1997 written by the Claimant to yourself?
2. If the answer to interrogatory 1 is yes, do you accept that you did not reply to it?
3. If the answer to interrogatory 2 is that you accept you did not reply to the letter, do you allege that you made any complaint or statement (written or oral) in response to receipt of the letter of 22 August 1997 to the effect that its content was inconsistent with the agreement you now allege of 8 August 1997, and if so, what complaint or statement did you make, to whom and when?

William Bliss, a Director of the above-named Respondent company, is required to answer all the above interrogatories.

Served this 23 November 1998, etc.

(Note: If these were questions from the arbitrator then the respondent would be DIRECTED to answer them—rather than required to by the claimant.)

Security for costs applications (see also p.77)

One of the commonest interlocutory applications is one by the respondent against the claimant for security for costs (s.38(3)) of defending the action. It is also the most common trigger for settlement, or the collapse, of an action.

Having said that, and despite its importance, I told Thomasina that I would not go into very much detail so far as security for costs applications are concerned. The reason is that it is a relatively complex procedure and our discussion was intended to explain the broad machinery of arbitration to her, in order that she could decide if she wished to undertake the necessary training to become an arbitrator. I would however run over the basics and show her a typical Order for Directions, which sets out the procedure for the parties to follow after I had received an application for security.

As a general rule, a successful respondent will ordinarily be awarded the costs which he has reasonably incurred in running his defence. Such an award will be of little value to him if it turns out that the claimant is unable to pay these costs, and thus, in some situations, it is reasonable for the arbitrator to order that the claimant provide security for some, or a substantial part, of the respondent's costs of defending the claim.

If one of the parties is unrepresented it may be necessary for the arbitrator to explain how that party should deal with (or make) such an application and what he, the arbitrator, expects from the parties and how he wishes to deal with the matter.

While the arbitrator may adopt any reasonable procedure to determine an application for security, provided he gives both parties the opportunity of making submissions, he must act judicially, and therefore it is submitted that he would do well to adopt a formal procedure.

He could remind the parties (particularly if they are legally represented) that he is not bound slavishly to follow the court's procedure but, nevertheless, he can usefully employ the guidelines applied by the court in dealing with applications for security—basically what he is interested in is whether a losing claimant could pay the respondent's costs of defending that claim, or, as it is defined in court proceedings, whether it can be established

"by credible testimony that there is reason to believe that the company will

158 What is this interlocutory period?

not be able to pay the defendant's costs if successful in his defence [, in which case the court may] require sufficient security to be given for those costs."

In order to establish this credible testimony the arbitrator would indicate to the parties in his Order for Directions (reproduced below) what documents he requires—in this case asking for a written application, together with a copy of a supporting affidavit served on the other side. After receiving the initial application and affidavit, the recipient party will serve an affidavit in reply, copied to the arbitrator. This affidavit will be accompanied by copies of all documents necessary to support the contention in that affidavit, i.e. annual accounts, bank statements, etc.

The arbitrator will need to satisfy himself that the amount of security required is reasonable and, as part of the supporting documentation, the respondent should provide a draft bill of the costs covering the amount for which they are seeking security. This bill will normally set out the time spent or to be spent by fee chargers engaged on the reference, together with the hourly rates which they are claiming. Depending upon the application the arbitrator may decide to order security for a shorter period than that sought by the application, leaving it to the applicant to make a further application at a later date, if appropriate.

Doesn't the arbitrator have to be something of a financial wizard to understand company accounts and balance sheets? asked Thomasina. No, I said. The arbitrator is not expected to be a financial expert, and if necessary, or if the accounts are complex, a separate affidavit could be attached from an accountant interpreting these financial statements. If this is not done and the arbitrator feels uncertain about his ability to determine the financial status of the party from the documents before him, he can inform the parties that he will take independent expert advice, telling the parties from whom he is seeking it, and giving them a chance to object to his choice. He will tell the parties that he will make available to them the advice that he has received and that he will make up his own mind, having considered this advice. Following this the arbitrator will hear the application at a short hearing.

Isn't this all a bit heavy? asked Thomasina. Not really, I said, for, if after receiving and considering the parties' submissions I decided to order security for the respondent's costs and the claimant was unable to provide it, he would be in danger of having his claim struck out. Thus, an arbitrator must treat all such applications extremely seriously.

Going back to the submissions, it is not sufficient that the applicant's accountant, for example, who is a credible witness, merely put forward the view of the claimant's inability to pay. If there is conflicting evidence the court (and therefore the arbitrator) must have regard to it. In particular, the court is not entitled to disregard the unchallenged evidence of the plaintiff's (claimant's) accountant as to its ability to pay costs.

One more thing, I said, that Thomasina should understand is that it is not only against a claimant that such an application can be made but also against a counterclaimant, i.e. where there is a substantial counterclaim the respondent could be asked to put up security for the claimant's costs of defending that counterclaim.

I then produced a typical order for directions setting out the procedure for the parties to follow subsequent to an application for security for costs from both parties where there is both a claim and a substantial counterclaim.

What is this interlocutory period?

Typical Direction for procedure for dealing with security for costs application

IN THE MATTER OF THE ARBITRATION ACT 1996

AND

IN THE MATTER OF AN ARBITRATION UNDER THE JCT 1998 EDITION OF THE CONSTRUCTION INDUSTRY MODEL ARBITRATION RULES

BETWEEN

RELIABLE BUILDERS LTD   Claimant

and

SANCTUARY HOUSE LTD   Respondent

ORDER FOR DIRECTIONS NO 18

Further to the Claimant's Application, 10 October 1998, and the Counter-Claimant's Application of the same date, for Security for their Costs, I exercise the power I have by virtue of clause 8 of my Terms and Conditions, signed by the Claimant on 26 November 1997 and by the Respondent on 23 December 1997; and the parties having made no agreement to the contrary, s.38(3) of the Arbitration Act 1996 applies.

ACCORDINGLY I HEREBY DIRECT as follows:

1.00 The claimant is to provide credible evidence to me by Affidavit, copied to the Respondent, showing why he believes that the Respondent will not be able to pay the Claimant's costs if the Claimant is successful in defending the Respondent's Counterclaim in this reference. This Affidavit to be served not later than 5.00 p.m. 21 November 1998.

2.00 The Respondent is to provide credible evidence to me by Affidavit, copied to the Claimant, showing why he believes that the Claimant will not be able to pay the Respondent's costs if the Respondent is successful in defending the Claim in this reference. This Affidavit to be served not later than 5.00 p.m. 21 November 1998.

3.00 Both Affidavits 1.00 and 2.00 above to state the amount

What sort of interlocutory directions? 161

of security required and to be accompanied by a skeleton make-up of costs showing the amount of the applying party's costs incurred to date and an estimate of their future costs.

4.00 Following receipt of these Affidavits the Claimant and the Respondent will serve on me, copied to the other side, not later than 5.00 p.m. 28 November 1998, an Affidavit in reply. Such Affidavits will be accompanied by copies of all documents necessary to support the contentions in that Affidavit i.e. annual accounts, bank statements etc.

5.00 If, on receipt of the Affidavit, in reply and supporting documentation, the financial position of either party is not absolutely clear to me from these documents then, on my request, that party will arrange for a separate Affidavit from an independent financial adviser, interpreting these financial statements.

6.00 In addition, or alternatively, on receipt of all Affidavits and supporting documents, I may then decide that I need independent assistance to interpret these documents prior to determining this issue. If I decide on this step I will inform the parties of the name of the person from whom I intend to take advice and give them 24 hours to agree or object. The reasonable costs incurred of consulting an independent expert will be reimbursed to me as part of my fees and expenses.

7.00 I shall hear the parties, or their representatives, on these respective applications, on 10 March 1997, at Jayrich Associates' offices at Swansea House, 48 Queens Road, Norwich, Norfolk. The Hearing will commence at 9.00 a.m. and continue, if necessary, until 5.30 p.m. with one hour recess for luncheon.

8.00 The parties' representatives have agreed that I may apply, but not be rigidly bound by, the guidelines given by Gibson LJ in *Keary Developments Ltd* v. *Tarmac Construction Ltd* [1995] 3 All ER 524 CA.

BY CONSENT the parties agree to divide the time available equally between them and to restrict the hearing of this matter to one day.

9.00 I shall embody my determination on this issue in an Order for Directions. In the same Order I shall include security for my own fees and expenses in accordance with clause 7 of my Terms and Conditions.

10.00 Should either party fail to provide such security as I may direct, either for my own fees and expenses or those of another party, then I may stay the proceedings until such Direction is

162 What is this interlocutory period?

complied with, with costs "thrown away" to be paid by the defaulting party in any event.

   11.00 Liberty to Apply.

   12.00 Costs in the reference.

D Mark Cato MSc FRICS FCIArb
Arbitrator

31 October 1998

To: Jayrich Associates	Representatives for the Claimant FAO Joel Redman
Kalmsyde & Joyoff	Solicitors for the Respondent FAO James Crighton

What sort of interlocutory directions? 163

Why did it take almost three weeks for you to issue this order for directions, following the parties' application to you? asked Thomasina. Quite simply, I said, because my first reaction to any such application is to invite the party to whom the request for security is addressed if it is prepared voluntarily to provide the security sought. It is only after I have received notification from that party that it is *not* prepared to provide the security requested that I resort to a formal direction.

So, you consider the parties' submissions and decide that one or the other (or both) are to provide security, said Thomasina. What happens if a party who has been directed by you to provide security does not do so? There is a specific provision for this in the Act (s.41(6)), I said. Following a party's failure to comply with my direction I would have to issue a peremptory order. If the party then fails to comply with that peremptory order I may make an award dismissing the claim (or counterclaim, if appropriate).

That's as far as I prepared to go with security for costs, I said. Let's look at some of the other common interlocutory applications.

Discovery (see Disclosure of Documents, p.67)

As I pointed out when we were considering the agenda items for the preliminary meeting, I rarely give an order for general discovery. Thus most applications for discovery or disclosure of documents are for specific discovery. The reason for this, I reminded Thomasina, was that with the Statement of Case procedure, the parties are directed to include copies of all principal documents on which reliance will be placed with their statements, plus a list of any documents that that party considers necessary to support in any part its statement.

Having provided a list of these documents to the other party, that party has a right to inspect and then copy any of those documents to which that party wishes to refer.

I then showed Thomasina a typical order for general discovery, embodied in a letter rather than a formal direction.

"I HEREBY DIRECT that each party will serve upon the other a list of files, in their power or possession, which are relevant to the issues in dispute, whether helpful or not to that party's case—the contents of which shall be clearly described. In particular all the documents mentioned in Jayrich

164 What is this interlocutory period?

Associates' letter 23 February 1999 in paragraph 12, and Kalmsyde & Joyoff's letter 28 February 1999 in paragraph 3 shall be included in these lists. Such lists to be exchanged not later than 5.00 p.m. 7 March 1999 with inspection thereafter on three working days' notice."

The reason I gave this order for general discovery, against my inclination, was because both parties wrote making a request for general discovery.

What do you do if one party or the other fails to comply with your order for general discovery? Thomasina asked. I would have to issue a Peremptory Order in the same terms as the previous order, warning that if the party continued its failure to comply then I may draw such adverse inference from the act of non-compliance as the circumstances justify, I said (s.41(7)(b)). What does that mean exactly? she said. Well, I could, for example, make a presumption in favour of a statement in the party's submission who had made the application for discovery, I replied.

Extensions of time

Extensions of time to comply with dates given in my orders for directions is another common application with which the arbitrator has to deal during this interlocutory period.

When I set the timetable at the preliminary meeting and, in particular, a date for a hearing (if appropriate), I always build in a little float time to allow for the possibility of an application or two for a short extension of time. If, however, a party fails seriously to comply with the timetable, and as such it causes the hearing dates to be postponed, unless it has good reason for that failure, it will find that it is ordered to pay "costs thrown away" as a result, in any event. In any event simply means that it will pay these costs whether it is the successful party or not. I reminded Thomasina that I gave this warning to the parties at the preliminary meeting.

Generally failing to comply with the arbitrator's directions

I have already indicated to Thomasina some of the powers that I have if a party fails to comply with any of my Peremptory Orders. In addition, I can direct that the party in default not be entitled to rely upon any allegation or material which was the subject matter of the order (s.41(7)(a)).

Alternatively, I can proceed to an award on the basis of such materials as have been properly provided (s.41(7)(c)), as well as having power to make such an order as I think fit as to the payment of costs incurred in consequence of non-compliance.

If I am having real problems with one of the parties, and I believe it is important for the fair outcome of the dispute for that party to comply with one of my Peremptory Orders, then, in the last resort, I could make an application to the court to order compliance (s.42). Alternatively, the party other than the one who is failing to comply can make the application to court with my consent. Once the court has ordered the party to comply if it continues its failure then, of course, it is in contempt of court with all that that implies.

Ex parte proceedings

The worst sort of non-compliance is when a respondent refuses to take any part in the proceedings (or any further part) and the arbitrator is obliged to proceed in the absence of that party, i.e. *ex parte*.

Some years ago I made an *aide memoire* for such *ex parte* situations. These notes are just as apposite today as they were when originally written, I told Thomasina. We then considered these notes.

1. Have you power to proceed "ex parte" (for example, under Rules)? [This power is now given to the arbitrator by section 41(4) AA '96 unless the parties agree otherwise.]
2. Burden of proof on attending party the same as if unrepresented party was present. If claimant, then must adduce evidence to satisfy you on claim, must deal with defence (if served) and counterclaim (if served). Must take into account any evidence or submissions which the absent party had previously put in.
3. Arbitrator must ensure that every Point of Claim and Counterclaim is satisfactorily dealt with by attending party. If minded not to accept evidence on a particular point then say so and why, otherwise could be misconduct (*Fox* v. *Wellfair*). [Now "serious irregularity", section 68.]

    Having said you are minded to reject evidence, say why and then give the attending party the opportunity to answer your objection and inform them whether you still reject or accept.

    But NOTE it is not the arbitrator's duty to protect the interests of the unrepresented party—you can only deal with the case as presented by the unrepresented party.

    Where the defence raises an issue of fact of which the respondent

has the burden of proof, if the respondent does not come forward to support his case the arbitrator can ignore it.
4. Strict rules of evidence must be applied in "ex parte" proceedings. Impartiality must be more apparent.
5. Write to the parties when your award is ready and inform them that you are ready to publish your award and will do so unless you hear from the parties within 14 days (i.e. give them a last opportunity to make representations to you).

What is this *Fox* v. *Wellfair* you keep mentioning? Thomasina said. I thought you promised that you would not cite cases to me at this stage. I agreed, but said that it is almost impossible to speak about *ex parte* proceedings and an arbitrator misconducting those proceedings (as it was called in those days) without reference to this milestone case. In due course, I suggested, she should read it for herself.

Having plunged into one case I sinned again and cited what Lord Denning said in another case, concerning the point that I made in paragraph 3 of these notes about the arbitrator not protecting a party's interests.

"The arbitrator should not do for the defendants what they could and should have done for themselves. His function is not to supply evidence for the defendants but to adjudicate upon the evidence given before him. He can and should use his special knowledge both to understand the evidence that is given—the letters that have been passed—the usage of the trade—the dealings of the market—and to appreciate the work of all that he sees upon a view. But he cannot use his special knowledge—or at any rate he should not use it—so as to provide evidence on behalf of the defendants which they have not chosen to provide for themselves. So then he would be discarding the role of an impartial arbitrator and assuming the role of advocate for the defaulting side. At any rate he should not use his own knowledge to derogate from the evidence of the plaintiffs' experts—without putting his own knowledge to them and giving them a chance of answering and showing that his own view was wrong."

Awards on different issues and partial awards

Before we leave the interlocutory process I ought to mention my power, unless the parties have agreed that I shall not have that power, to make what used to be called interim awards on various issues (s.47). This can be a very good cost-effective way of running an arbitration provided the award finally disposes of the subject matter of that award. It is a useful way, for example, of dealing with a preliminary issue.

These awards must be distinguished from what the Act calls provisional awards (s.39). Although the Act refers to provisional awards, it is considered that this section should more properly be termed provisional orders, as it specifically contemplates orders which are subject to later adjustment, whereas awards, unless agreed otherwise, are final and binding in their effect (s.58(1)).

The power to make a provisional order is a very important new power that the arbitrator enjoys under the Act. He can, for instance, order the payment of money between the parties or make an order for an interim payment on account of the costs of the arbitration. In this manner the arbitrator can redress the balance between an impecunious claimant, whose impecuniosity has been caused or may have been caused by the withholding of monies by the respondent, and that respondent.

If a respondent was taking advantage of its financial muscle to withhold money that was probably rightfully due to the claimant, then the making of such a provisional order will often lead to an early settlement.

Pre-hearing review (see p.69)

Usually one of the last interlocutory matters is the pre-hearing review, I said, although this will usually only take place in the larger cases. I reminded Thomasina of the preliminary meeting agenda which set out the sorts of matters which are dealt with at such a meeting. For example, I consider all outstanding issues which need to be narrowed and clarified. I may question whether any of these issues may be worth pursuing.

I will consider with the parties the order in which the witnesses are to be called and the how the reference shall be conducted.

I check to see whether all of my directions have been complied with or whether there is a need for any fresh directions. In other words, it is a final mopping-up before the main hearing, and it usually takes place a month or so before the scheduled date for the commencement of that hearing.

This talk earlier about the parties failing to comply with the arbitrator's directions had whetted Thomasina's appetite. What do you do, she said, if you get thoroughly fed up with the parties? Can

168 What is this interlocutory period?

you just walk away and leave them to it? Also, what happens if the parties want to get rid of you? She hastened to assure me that she realised that could not apply in my case but, she said, there must be some incompetent arbitrators about!

This flood of questions came late in the afternoon, so I suggested to Thomasina that we had had enough for one day but I would certainly go into these questions and some of the other few remaining outstanding points at our next session.

I excused myself on the totally valid ground that I really ought to take a final look through an award that I had drafted earlier that day. Thomasina then left with a promise from me of an early resumption.

CHAPTER 8

MORE ON THE ARBITRATOR

At our next meeting, a week or two later, I told Thomasina that I would pick up from our last session and tell her about how an arbitrator extricates himself from an uncomfortable reference and how parties get rid of an incompetent arbitrator. However, before I did so, I told her that I wished to deal in a little more depth with two matters on which we had touched briefly before: the adversarial/inquisitorial process, and the use of the arbitrator's own expertise.

ADVERSARIAL OR INQUISITORIAL PROCESS?

By now, I said, I hoped that Thomasina appreciated that the normal process followed in arbitration was an adversarial one. That is, each side has the opportunity of presenting its case and defending the case made against it. This process is conducted through examination, cross-examination and re-examination of witnesses, carried out by the opposing parties' advocates. The arbitrator will then make his determination on the basis of the evidence that he has heard. Generally speaking he will rely on the parties' advocates to extract the evidence; however, he will of course intervene, usually at the end of each process of examination, to ask questions of his own. Normally, however, an arbitrator would not go beyond seeking answers to such questions in order to clarify some piece of evidence or other.

Did she recall my mentioning Sherlock Holmes in discussing the arbitrator's powers, when we went through the preliminary meeting agenda? I asked. She did, she said, but to be honest she had not really understood what I was getting at.

170 More on the arbitrator

One of the primary objectives of AA '96, I said, was to give the arbitrator the greatest possible flexibility in relation to the resolution of disputes referred to him, in order to achieve a cost-effective and speedy solution. One of the ways in which the Act provides for this is to give the arbitrator power to take the initiative in ascertaining the facts and the law—to act inquisitorially—provided the parties do not agree otherwise (s.34(2)(g)). In other words, the Act provides for the arbitrator to determine

"whether and to what extent the tribunal should itself take the initiative in ascertaining the facts and the law."

This means, I said, that the arbitrator himself can ask questions, whether by written request or orally. Alternatively, he can consent to one party or the other asking such questions or seeking admissions as to facts if he is convinced that by doing so costs will be saved through shortening the hearing time.

As the parties rarely agree on anything, since the enactment of AA '96 I have invariably been given this power by default. In two references, the parties have approached me, during the interlocutory period, with a request that I use this inquisitorial power to investigate certain technical issues.

My earlier reference to Sherlock Holmes was meant to emphasise to Thomasina that I did not see it as the function of the arbitrator to act like an investigating magistrate might in France, for example. In other words I did not see it as the arbitrator's role to go out into the field, so to speak, seeking supporting evidence for one party's case or the other. Rather, I saw it as pro-active role in the process—both during the interlocutory phase and at the hearing.

I could best demonstrate to her, I said, by giving an example. Almost all construction disputes involve disagreement over variations, both as to quantum and liability. There are frequently schedules of defects which are also in dispute, again as to quantum and liability. It is my practice to have these items Scott Scheduled. I then suggest to the parties' representatives that I should meet their experts—usually quantity surveyors—to go through these schedules, item by item, prior to the hearing, in order to narrow the issues. Preferably their quantity surveyors will have authority to agree at least quantum, or, in some cases, quantum and liability.

Having disposed completely of some of the items on the Scott Schedule—if this is what the quantity surveyors are authorised to

Adversarial or inquisitorial process? 171

do—we will then agree what that quantum would be, subject to liability, for the remaining items, as well as identifying the witnesses who will give evidence on this liability at the hearing.

Having agreed the extent of the parties' representatives' authority in my meetings with them alone, I would take an active part in the determination of quantum of these items on the Scott Schedule. Normally the parties' representatives will agree a quantum figure between themselves, having listened to my comments. In the event that they cannot agree then I determine the quantum for that item there and then, and the amount is then recorded on the Scott Schedule.

I believe this is a demonstration of the type of inquisitorial process that the authors of the Act had in mind. It has the merit of shortening the expensive hearing time through narrowing the issues. The main thing for arbitrators to remember, when exercising this inquisitorial power, is their overriding duty in section 33. In other words they must give all parties a reasonable opportunity of commenting on any initiative that they take to procure evidence.

Returning to the distinction between adversarial and inquisitorial procedures, I could do no better, I said, than to quote Lord Mustill on the difference between these two systems. Under the adversarial system:

"... the procedural initiative lies mainly with the parties ... the arbitrator does not and cannot call witnesses himself; he may ask them questions, but the eliciting of the evidence is primarily a matter for the parties.

This is not to suggest that the role of the arbitrator is merely supine. On the contrary, a good arbitrator will stamp his personality on the proceedings in such a way as to insure that the proceedings are conducted with the minimum of effort, delays and expense. Nevertheless it remains broadly true that his task is to make a choice between alternatives presented to him, rather than to strike out on a course of his own."

Lord Mustill says that the essence of the inquisitorial system is:

"... that the tribunal takes the initiative, in an endeavour to find the truth. Under the adversarial procedure, the arbitrator plays a less active role. Naturally, he wishes to ascertain the truth, but instead of searching for it, he allows it to evolve from a kind of dialectic between the parties, the assumption being that if it is left to the parties to present the alternative versions of the true position, they will between them furnish the arbitrator with sufficient material upon which to base an informed decision."

I could certainly not improve on what Lord Mustill says of

these processes but would add the following note of caution to the inquisitorial arbitrator. When putting questions to the parties, they should be made in as neutral a manner as the arbitrator is able. He should be more circumspect about putting questions dealing with issues of fact rather than questions dealing with matters of opinion. If he is an author, he should be satisfied that the parties are aware of his published views that may have a bearing on the matter in hand. Finally, he should put the parties on notice where he is troubled by a lack of evidence or submissions in the particular area.

All this so far concerns acting inquisitorially in connection with ascertaining the facts. When it comes to ascertaining the law, as a general rule, I would suggest to Thomasina that non-legally qualified arbitrators avoided the temptation. The only time that I believe it may be reasonable for the arbitrator to get involved in ascertaining the law might be in certain cases where neither party is legally represented and he has some knowledge of a legal point which he believes could influence the outcome of the case. Under such circumstances, it would be perfectly reasonable for him to state his understanding of the law and, as a result, his understanding of the effect of that law on the facts of the case and to leave it to the parties to take advice on this if they saw fit. Having done so, then the arbitrator would be perfectly entitled to come to his decision on the basis of his own understanding of the law. Beyond that I believe it would be unwise to go.

USE OF OWN EXPERTISE

As I said earlier in our discussion, an arbitrator is usually appointed for his expertise in the subject matter of the dispute. Thus, shipping people are usually appointed arbitrators in maritime cases; commodity brokers in disputes concerning commodities, etc.

Thus, it may well be that the arbitrator knows more about the nature, as opposed to the particular facts, of the dispute than the parties. If he knows something from his own experience which will have an influence on his ultimate decision, then he should disclose this to the parties and give them the opportunity of commenting on it. In other words, he must not take "secret evidence" from himself, otherwise he could subsequently find his award being challenged on the ground of serious irregularity with all the unhappy consequences that could entail (s.68).

The classic example of an arbitrator who ignored this simple advice is to be seen in the case to which I referred Thomasina earlier, that of *Fox* v. *Wellfair*.

ARBITRATOR—RESIGNATION OR TERMINATION?

As promised at the end of our last session, I said I would now deal with the question of the dissatisfied or unsatisfactory arbitrator.

Resignation

While I can scarcely envisage a situation occurring in which I would feel constrained to resign from a reference, unless I was requested to do so by both parties, the possibility of doing so is now open to an arbitrator through the Act (s.25).

AA '96 makes provision for the parties to agree with an arbitrator on the consequences of his resignation regarding his entitlement to fees and expenses and any liability thereby incurred by him. If there is no such agreement by the parties, then if an arbitrator wishes to resign he may, after giving notice to the parties, apply to the court to grant him relief from any liability and to make such orders as the court sees fit regarding his entitlement to fees and expenses. One such example of where the court is likely to relieve the arbitrator from any liability is if he has to resign on the ground of ill health or, say, family bereavement.

So this new power, I said, is a two-edged weapon, on the one hand giving an arbitrator the opportunity to extricate himself from a situation in which he is not happy, but leaving him open to the consequences of his action. For example, if the court thought him unreasonable in resigning, it could order that he forfeit his fees, or refund fees already paid, or, presumably, even order in extreme cases that he should be liable for some of the costs thrown away by his action in resigning. A sobering thought, I said.

Termination

We have seen how an arbitrator can resign if he finds the reference un-conducive, but what if one or the other party considers the arbitrator incompetent or biased and wishes to have him removed?

Before AA '96, in order to have an arbitrator removed a party had to show to the court's satisfaction that he had misconducted himself or the proceedings. This unfortunate term has now been substituted by the expression "serious irregularity" (s.68).

This is a complex matter, I told Thomasina, which frankly I do not believe we should go into in any great depth. But to answer your question, the parties acting together can agree to revoke the arbitrator's authority, or it can even be done by the appointing body, presumably on application of one or other of the parties (s.23). So this would be a means of removing the arbitrator without involving the court where, for example, both parties agreed that the arbitrator simply was not capable of conducting the proceedings.

More often than not it is one party (rather than both) who complains about the conduct of the arbitrator and seeks to have him removed. Under these circumstances that dissatisfied party would have to give notice to the other party and the arbitrator and then apply to the court. Impartiality or bias are common reasons. There is a new ground, however, under the Act, and that is where the arbitrator has refused or failed properly to conduct the proceedings or to use reasonable dispatch in conducting the proceedings or making an award *and* that substantial injustice has been, or will be, caused to the applicant (s.24). This is an interesting ground as it reflects the duty laid on arbitrators under section 33 to conduct the proceedings expeditiously.

We will consider what happens when an arbitrator is removed as a result of an appeal against his award when we consider appeals, a little later on our discussion, I told Thomasina. (See p.209.)

IMMUNITY OF ARBITRATOR

Isn't all this talk of liability rather alarming? said Thomasina. Surely judges are not at risk, why so then arbitrators? Who would want to take the risk? she said. It's not as bad as that, I said. Apart from the possibility of liability in the event of an unreasonable resignation, an arbitrator is not liable for anything he does or omits to do when discharging his function as arbitrator unless the act or omission is shown to have been in bad faith, for example involving malice or dishonesty.

FEES AND HOW TO GET THEM PAID

The best way to ensure that there is no problem over your fees, I told Thomasina, is to get them agreed at the onset. We spent some considerable time looking at my Terms and Conditions earlier in our discussion (p.80), and provided both parties have signed such terms, or something similar, then the arbitrator should experience no difficulty over the amount of such fees. If he is prudent, or at all concerned about the parties' ability to discharge these fees, then he can invoke the discretion given to him to submit interim fee claims. If such an interim application remains unpaid, then, depending on the state of the reference, he can reasonably stay the proceedings until he has been paid.

We considered earlier the arbitrator's power to order security for costs (s.38) (pp.77, 101 and 157). As the Act makes no distinction between the arbitrator's costs and those of the parties, provided the arbitrator has this power then he may exercise it in relation to his own costs. Again, a prudent arbitrator will ask for such security in advance of a long hearing.

A further safeguard exists for the arbitrator under the Act, which give him the right to refuse to deliver an award to the parties except upon payment of his fees and expenses (s.56).

The Act also makes clear what has always been thought to be the position, that the parties are jointly and severally liable to pay the arbitrator's reasonable fees and expenses (s.28). This then covers the situation where the parties have refused to sign his terms, or the arbitrator has been appointed prior to his Terms and Conditions being agreed and has merely informed the parties what they are.

What happens, said Thomasina, if the parties complete the reference and the arbitrator informs them that his award is ready for collection on payment of his outstanding fees and the parties consider those fees are unreasonable—they want the award but are not prepared to pay the amount of fees demanded? The Act makes provision for this situation, I said (s.28(2)). Either party may apply to the court after giving notice to the other party and the arbitrator, and the court may order that the amount of these fees be adjusted by such means and upon such terms as the court may direct. Under these circumstances, the court also has power to order the arbitrator to refund any amount of fees already paid to him (s.28(2)).

In all situations where the court is asked to consider the reasonableness of the arbitrator's fees and expenses (if any), the arbitrator has the right to make a submission to court or to be heard.

If all else fails and the parties refuse to pay the arbitrator his reasonable fees, then he too can resort to the court by suing the parties. Fortunately, arbitrators rarely have to resort to this draconian measure.

CHAPTER 9

THE COURT'S ROLE IN ARBITRAL PROCEEDINGS*

It is said that the court's powers are broadly confined to those which support the arbitral process. The Act contains a limited list of the circumstances under which the court could intervene, but this is generally narrower than the court's power in litigation (s.44). Typically, this power includes such matters as the taking of evidence of the witnesses, the preservation of evidence and the granting of interim injunctions. Even these powers will not be exercised unless the court is satisfied that the arbitrator has no power with regard to the matter with which it is being asked to deal.

Areas other than those which we have already considered in which the court may act (provided the parties have not agreed otherwise) to support the arbitral process include:

- a failure of the appointment procedure (s.18/19);
- the determination of any question as to the substantive jurisdiction of the arbitral tribunal (s.32);
- the court's power to enforce the arbitrator's Peremptory Orders (s.42). I reminded Thomasina that we had already considered this (p.164). The Act also permits the court to supplement the sanctions available to the arbitrator by applying those sanctions which are available to the court for a breach of court order. For example, the court could fine a party or send him to prison for contempt.

The committee drafting the Act said of this power (s.42):

"In our view there may well be circumstances where, in the interests of justice, the fact that the court has sanctions which in the nature of things

* See p.209, Appeals To The Court.

cannot be given to the arbitrators (e.g. committal to prison for contempt) will assist the proper functioning of the arbitral process."

Interestingly, the parties are able to agree that the court does not enjoy this power, but if they make no such agreement then the power can only be invoked at the behest of the arbitrator or by one of the parties with the arbitrator's permission:

- a power to secure the attendance before the tribunal of a witness in order to give oral testimony or to produce documents or other material evidence (s.43). The Act provides for a party to use the same procedure as a court to enforce the attendance of a witness or the production of documents, i.e. subpoenas;
- a power that the court may, on the application of the party and the upon notice to the other party, determine any questions of law arising in the course of the proceedings which the court is satisfied substantially affect the rights of one or more of the parties (s.45);
- provision for the court to extend the time for making an award (subject to certain conditions) where this is limited by, or in pursuance of, the arbitration agreement (s.50);
- that an award may be enforced in the same manner as a judgment or order of the court to the same effect (s.66);
- the right of a party to apply to the court to challenge an award as to the arbitrator's substantive jurisdiction or the lack of it (s.67);
- the right of a party to challenge the award on the ground of serious irregularity (s.68). I told Thomasina that we would consider this section in more depth when we came to look at appeals at the end of our discussion (see p.209);
- the right of a party to appeal to the court on a question of law arising out of the award (s.69). Like the last item, it again will be considered the more depth later (see p.209);
- power for the court to order the tribunal to state the reasons for its award in sufficient detail to enable the court to properly consider an appeal (s.70).

Basically, I told Thomasina, that was all I was going to say about the court's role in arbitration. Of course much has been written on the subject and, if and when she gets involved in arbitration, of course she will need to go deeper into this aspect. The main thing for her to remember at this stage is that there is generally a policy of non-intervention by the courts.

Although the last half-dozen of the court's powers which I have listed deal with the award, the bulk of them cover situations which could occur during the interlocutory process.

This then, I said, takes us neatly to what is usually the final act in any arbitration: the hearing.

CHAPTER 10

THE HEARING*

We considered a number of matters on which the parties' agreement is necessary in connection with the hearing when we discussed the agenda for the preliminary meeting (see p.50). These, then, were matters which we considered right at the beginning of the reference. What Thomasina wanted to know was how does the arbitrator himself prepare for the hearing?

Having ascertained that suitable accommodation has been booked, the arbitrator must confirm the date, time and venue for the hearing through an order for directions.

His earliest order directed that the hearing bundle, advocates' opening submissions, witness statements, expert reports and highlighted authorities all be delivered to him seven days before the scheduled commencement of the hearing. The reason for this, I told Thomasina, was that any arbitrator worth his salt would adequately prepare for a hearing. Depending upon the size, complexity and nature of the dispute, the reading time alone can cover several days. I make a point of physically setting aside time at the beginning, prior to the commencement of the hearing, specifically for this purpose.

If there is a pre-hearing review, at that review meeting I ask the parties to let me know what they wish me to read in preparation for the hearing. If it is a relatively small dispute the answer is usually all of the hearing bundle, but if it is a large and complex dispute involving tens or even hundreds of files, the arbitrator will almost certainly have ordered a core bundle of documents, and it is usually this core bundle which he will be requested to read prior to the hearing.

---

*See p.69.

My main objective, through this preparatory reading, is to attempt to identify the issues in dispute and gain a general understanding of the parties' opposing stances in relation to these issues. This means reading, among other things, the "pleadings" (the parties' Statements of Case and Replies), all of the witness statements, the experts' reports and any legal argument.

Why bother to have the hearing at all? said Thomasina. Surely you could make up your mind on the strength of what you have read and save the expense of the hearing, she said. Of course, I replied, you're right. Small disputes can often be reasonably resolved through "documents only". However, the parties need to know this from the inception in order to ensure that they have fully pleaded their case in their statements and submissions. Where the parties are aware that there is to be a hearing, some of the strength of their case will be made by breaking down evidence of the opposing party's witnesses by cross-examination.

Put another way, basically, through this pre-reading exercise, the arbitrator is attempting to familiarise himself with the background to the dispute. For this reason, as part of this overall exercise, I invariably draft the preliminary recitals of my award, the very first section of which is headed "Background to the Dispute". By tracing the chronology of the dispute and having to commit this to writing I find that I have a far better understanding of what the dispute is all about than I would have otherwise.

How could you start drafting your award before you've even heard the evidence? asked Thomasina. The whole of the award up to the substantive part where the arbitrator starts to make his findings can reasonably be drafted prior to the hearing, I told her. There are no decisions in this part of the award, merely a statement of the facts that led to the dispute. The arbitrator has all this information at his fingertips at this stage, or should have if his preparation has been thorough, so why not set it down and give himself a flying start with the award following the conclusion of the hearing? I asked her.

When I have identified the main issues of claim (and counterclaim, if any) I allocate a colour to each of them. I then colour code the pleadings (Statements), the witness statements, the experts' reports and the legal authorities using the same code. I prepare an index at the front of the notebook, in which I intend to record the evidence at the hearing, with as many columns as there are issues, again with the same colour noted against the menu. At the end of each hearing day, I mark the margin against the evidence that I have heard, using the same colour code, and record the page number of that piece of evidence in the index of my book.

In this way, when I come to consider each issue at the conclusion of the hearing I merely need to follow through with one colour at a time. I stressed to Thomasina that this is my personal way of doing things. Other arbitrators have their own systems which, I have no doubt, are equally effective. All I can say is that my system seems to work for me.

So the preparation is over and you arrive at the hearing venue: what next? she said. Well, I said, even before I leave the office I go through a checklist for the hearing: glasses; coloured pens; the Old and the New Testaments; a ruler, among other things; as well as my colour-coded copies of the documents. It is very easy to forget to take something important like your glasses and find yourself handicapped on the first day, so what better than your checklist, I said.

OK, I have arrived at the hearing. I usually try to get there at least 20 minutes before the scheduled time for commencement, I said. If I have one or two pupils present they will have to be briefed. I need to check that the room has been laid out properly and that the microphones are in place and working. I need to set up my files in stands so that they are readily accessible to me and I do not slow down the proceedings by hunting for documents to which I am referred. By now the clock will have run its course and the time for the commencement of the hearing will have arrived.

The first thing I do is to record the names of those present. I will usually reiterate any agreement that we have made previously, probably at the pre-hearing review, concerning the conduct of the hearing, so that the parties' representatives can alert their witnesses.

I will then deal with general "housekeeping" matters, i.e. the time when I intend to break for coffee, tea; what arrangements have been made for lunch; what retirement rooms there are, and so on.

Next, I will ask the parties' representatives, particularly if they are represented by counsel, if they have any applications they wish to make. Even at this late stage there may be applications to amend pleadings, to introduce fresh evidence etc., but usually I will have had prior notice of such applications. Otherwise the non-applying party may request an adjournment to consider the application, which I would find difficult to resist.

At this stage I will receive a list of the issues, hopefully agreed between the parties and, if appropriate, envelopes containing any sealed offers to settle (see p.68). After that, the claimant will open his case. If he has engaged counsel then he will do it with counsel's opening submission, which, of course, I have already read, having received it in writing. Having said that, I always give counsel the opportunity to enlarge briefly on this opening if he wishes, following which he will call his first witness. Again, having read all the proofs of evidence, after I have administered the oath and, with the consent of the witness, taken a Polaroid photograph of him, I invite counsel to take over, I told Thomasina.

Photograph the witness? said Thomasina, incredulously, what on earth for? If you ever find yourself sitting on a case with, say, up to 24 witnesses, you may experience difficulty in remembering precisely which witness gave what evidence, when you come to review it in writing your award, I said. By pasting a photograph of that witness in your notebook at the beginning of his or her cross-examination that evidence comes to life. This is a tip that I thoroughly recommended Thomasina to adopt if she ever became a practising arbitrator.

The claimant's counsel, having called his first witness, will ask him to identify his proof and confirm that he stands by it, i.e. does not wish to change anything in it. Having done so, that witness will be handed straight over to the opposing advocate for cross-examination, following which he may be re-examined by his own advocate to clarify some answers extracted in cross-examination.

Well, that's it, basically, I said. We work our way through all of the claimant's witnesses of fact and then the respondent's. Having said that, I have varied this recently by swearing in several witnesses of fact from each side and hearing all the evidence on a particular issue, thus disposing of it once and for all in one fell swoop. This only really works, I said, in the smaller cases.

Certainly this is the way I deal with the experts, even in the bigger cases. The great advantage, I said, of swearing in experts of a like discipline and having them examined on discrete issues one after the other is that a comparison of the evidence between the experts is made much easier.

The important thing to remember, I told Thomasina, was to warn counsel of your intention to call these experts together so that they can properly prepare their cross-examination. The main task facing the arbitrator is to keep control of the proceedings and to deal firmly and reasonably quickly with any objections or applications from counsel or the party's advocate, if the party is not legally represented.

Quite apart from taking a full note of the proceedings, despite the back-up of the tape recording, the arbitrator will have to note, on the blank page opposite his note, any questions that he wishes to put to that witness at the end of his re-examination. Where counsel is involved, such questions should be left to this stage. If the parties are not represented, the arbitrator can usefully take a more pro-active role in the questioning process, sometimes coming close to cross-examination. If he does so, however, I said, he must take care to give the opposing advocate, or lay party, the opportunity of cross-examining the witness on any point that he has put to that witness.

After all the witnesses and the experts have been fully examined, first the respondent's advocate and then the claimant's advocate will sum up briefly. I say briefly, I told Thomasina, because you will recall that I directed that the closing submissions should be submitted to me in writing following the conclusion of the hearing. Sometimes, in the more complex cases where counsel is instructed, they will often request an opportunity to make an oral submission, following their written submissions to the arbitrator, a week or so after the conclusion of the hearing. Depending upon the nature and complexity of the dispute and perhaps the legal issues involved, I would usually accede to this request.

All that remains then is for the arbitrator to write his award.

CHAPTER 11

WET TOWEL TIME—WRITING THE AWARD*

The hearing is over and you're back in your office with several notebooks full of evidence; the parties' submissions; their pleadings; and the advocates' closing submissions, all neatly colour-coded as we discussed, I said. Are you then ready to write your award? I asked rhetorically.

Not quite. First, you find the facts and then consider the parties' submissions on law, analysing and then coming to a decision on those points of law. You then apply holdings of law to the facts and your decisions will flow naturally.

Put more simply, I said, you consider the factual evidence you have heard and relate that evidence to each item in dispute and, as a result, make a finding of fact on that item. Following this, you must decide on liability for each point in dispute and then determine quantum.

How then to consider liability? I asked. Thomasina looked a bit blank. I had forgotten that I was speaking to someone with little or no knowledge of contract law, so I continued. It is necessary to carry out a basic analysis. For our purposes I will assume we are under contract, although the analysis for liability in tort is dealt with in the same way.

If the parties were legally represented, their advocates would almost certainly have taken you through a process on the following lines:

- Was there a contract?
- Was there a breach of contract?
- If there was a breach did any damage flow from the breach?

* See p.74.

- If the answer is yes—then are the damages a natural consequence of that breach?
- If so, was that breach foreseeable?
- If so, has the quantum been proved?
- If so, then that point of claim succeeds.

If the answer to any of those questions is no then the point fails. This is easier to understand in chart form, I said, producing one that I use in my lectures (see opposite).

Having dealt with liability for each issue, then you should move on to the next item in dispute, as identified by you when you constructed your index, I said.

These, then, are the basic principles or matters that should be considered in dealing with a claim for damages, but I stressed that this is not a process that the arbitrator goes through of his own volition. These are matters that arise out of evidence. It is not for the arbitrator to sit there dreaming up aspects of a party's claim or counterclaim. Therefore, I am not suggesting that you sit down and ask yourself all these questions if they have not been raised by either the parties or their representatives, I told Thomasina. Although, if any of them are in your mind when you come to consider the issues at the beginning of a hearing, or indeed at any stage during the hearing, you should inform the advocates and invite them to address you on your particular point of concern, I told her.

If, on the other hand, the parties are unrepresented and have no knowledge of the law, you may well have to go through this analysis from the evidence that they have produced, explaining the processes to the parties and inviting them to comment, as best they can, on your findings.

So there you are, what could be simpler than that? I said. That's the easy bit, and up to now you have not written a single word of your award, but you have decided on liability and on each point of claim and each point of counterclaim.

Now you should work out the actual quantum of damages for each of these points, including, where appropriate, interest and VAT.

The measure of damages to be applied is really beyond the scope of our discussion, I told Thomasina, but I shall be happy to go through this with you, if and when you get that far in your studies. That is, assuming, after all this, you decide that you would like to become an arbitrator. For the time being however, let us assume that

Flow chart analysing point of claim/counterclaim

FLOW CHART SHOWING HOW TO ANALYSE A POINT OF CLAIM OR COUNTERCLAIM

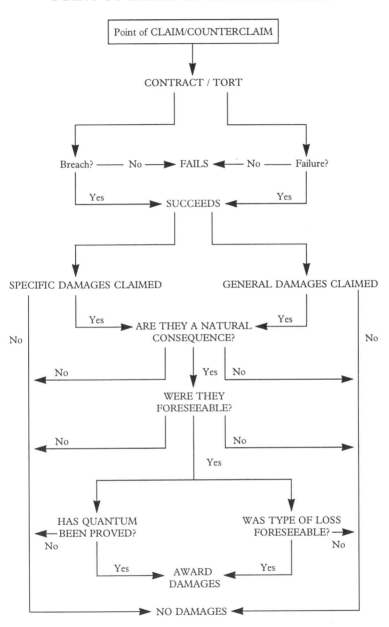

you have considered all the evidence and authorities and decided on liability and quantum for each and every item in dispute.

THE DRAFTING OF THE AWARD

Now we come to the drafting of the award itself, I said to Thomasina. The first thing I want to stress is that there are no fixed rules or guidelines covering this process—your way will be as good as my way—in the same way as we saw earlier that there is no set format for a reasoned award, but there are some fundamental requirements which must be observed.

I reminded her that we had already discussed *what is a reasoned award* (see p.74) and suggested that, before looking at the structure of the award, we first consider briefly what the essential requirements of a valid award are.

THE ESSENTIALS OF A VALID AWARD

As a student, I told her, I had devised a totally meaningless mnemonic to remind myself of these essentials—FACTS DO CANCEL.

With a minimum of amendment to cater for the new Act, this mnemonic still works today, as follows:

*F*inal—it must not leave any point partly or completely undecided (s.58(2)(1)).

*A*bsolutely certain—the parties must know what the arbitrator's decision is. For example, if a sum of money has to be paid, who has to pay it, to whom and by when (s.68(2)(f))?

*C*omply with the submission—if the submission to arbitration was to deal with liability and quantum and the award merely deals with liability, then it does not comply with the submission. Also comply with any special directions, i.e. time, place and manner of publication (s.68(2)(d)).

*T*ime—within prescribed time, if any. If no time prescribed then within a reasonable time (s.24(1)(d)(ii)).

*S*eat—state seat of the arbitration (s.52(5)).

*D*ate—must state the date when the award is made and be

signed by all the arbitrators or those assenting to the award (s.52(3) and (5)).

*O*ral—not oral; must be written unless the parties have agreed otherwise (s.52(3)) and comply with any requirement as to the form of the award (s.68(2)(h)).

*C*onsistent in all of its parts—not contradictory or ambiguous (s.68(2)(f)).

*A*ll matters disposed of—where there may be a multiplicity of items, such as in construction disputes, it is essential that all are disposed of (s.68(2)(d)).

*N*ot deal with matters not referred to, i.e. not pleaded—it may be that the claim is against one party who has an agent; unless it is part of the reference, the arbitrator shall not make a finding *vis-à-vis* the party to his agent (s.68(2)(b)).

*C*ontain reasons—unless it is agreed award or the parties have agreed to dispense with reasons (s.52(4)).

*E*xecutable—for example, cannot order party to enter neighbour's land without permission.

*L*egal—award cannot order something which is contrary to the law.

Now, I said, this is the exciting part—putting pen to paper.

THE STRUCTURE AND CONTENT OF THE AWARD

First, the cover. I think presentation is all important, I said. A well laid out and neatly bound award gives the parties reading it a degree of confidence in the arbitrator, even if the award itself is not as sound as it might be! So, first, we have a good cover, then we start on the first page with IN THE MATTER OF THE ARBITRATION ACT 1996 etc., giving the names of the parties, claimant and respondent, and describing what sort of award it is, whether FINAL—SAVE AS TO COSTS etc.

The first section I deal with is the BACKGROUND TO THE DISPUTE. It is clearly a very important part of the award as it sets out the backcloth against which your determination is made, I said, and it should be sufficiently clear to enable others not familiar with the case to learn in a few words what the dispute is all about.

I commended Thomasina to read some of Lord Denning's judgments for this part of the exercise. He was an excellent storyteller and I reminded her that we had read what he said about the thinking behind his judgments when we had touched on reasoned awards when we were considering the agenda for the preliminary meeting.

Now we considered two classic examples of Lord Denning's inimitable style. The first is from *Lloyds Bank Limited* v. *Bundy*, where he said:

"Broadchalke is one of the most pleasing villages in England. Old Herbert Bundy, the defendant, was a farmer. His home was Yew Tree Farm. It went back 300 years. His family had been there for generations. It was his only asset. But he did a very foolish thing. He mortgaged it to the bank. Up to the hilt. Not to borrow money for himself but for the sake of his son. Now the bank has come down on him. They have foreclosed. They want to get him out of Yew Tree Farm and sell it. They have brought this action against him for possession. Going out means ruin for him. He was granted Legal Aid. His lawyers put in a defence. They said that, when he executed the Charge to the bank, he did not know what he was doing: or at any rate that the circumstances were such that he ought not to be bound by it. At the trial his plight was plain. The judge was sorry for him. He said he was a 'poor old gentleman'.

He was so obviously incapacitated that the judge admitted his proof in evidence. He had a heart attack in the witness box. Yet the judge felt he could do nothing for him. 'There is nothing' he said, 'which takes this case out of the vast range of commercial transactions.' He ordered Herbert Bundy to give up possession of Yew Tree Farm to the bank. Now there is an Appeal to this Court. The ground is that the circumstances are so exceptional that Herbert Bundy should not be held bound. . . . Gathering all together, I would suggest that through all these instances there runs a single thread. They rest on 'inequality of bargaining power'.

By virtue of it, the English law gives relief to one who, without independent advice, enters into a contract upon terms which are very unfair or transfers property for a consideration which is grossly inadequate, when his bargaining power is grievously impaired by reason of his own needs or desires, or by his own ignorance or infirmity, coupled with undue influence or issues brought to bear on him by or for the benefit of others."

The other example is from *Beswick* v. *Beswick*:

"Old Peter Beswick was a coal merchant in Eccles, Lancashire. He had no business premises. All he had was a lorry, scales and weights. He used to take the lorry to the yard of the National Coal Board, where he bagged coal and took it round to his customers in the neighbourhood. His nephew, John Joseph Beswick, helped him in the business. In March 1962, old Peter Beswick and his wife were both over seventy. He had his leg amputated and was not in good health. The nephew was anxious to get hold of the business before the old man died. So they went to a solicitor, Mr Ashcroft,

The structure and content of the award 193

who drew up an agreement for them. The business was to be transferred to the nephew: old Peter Beswick was to be employed in it as a consultant for the rest of his life at £6–10–0 a week.

After his death the nephew was to pay his widow an annuity of £5 a week which was to come out of the business. After the agreement was signed, the nephew took over the business and ran it. The old man seemed to have found it difficult at first to adjust to the new situation, but he settled down. The nephew paid him £6–10–0 a week but, as expected, he did not live long. He died on 3 November 1963. His widow was 74 years of age in failing health. The nephew paid her the first £5. But then stopped paying her and has refused to pay her any more...".

This may not be the most perfect English. Indeed, some of Lord Denning's sentences are rather short on verbs, but at least, at the end of it, you are in no doubt what the dispute is all about.

Next THE WORKS. Briefly describe what was the subject matter of the contract. For example, the mechanical and electrical installation of the project situated at....

Then identify the form of CONTRACT and the arbitration clause in that contract.

Next your APPOINTMENT—say how you came to be appointed.

Follow that with INTERLOCUTORIES AND HEARING and spell out all the interlocutory processes that led up to and included the hearing. This is particularly important in an *ex parte* situation or where a party may attempt to have you removed, or your award set aside for any form of "serious irregularity" (see Post-award, p.209).

After you have dealt with the background in the dispute you can then say, I, the said THOMASINA NASTASIA TYRO, having read and considered the evidence and submissions, by and on behalf of both parties, HEREBY MAKE AND PUBLISH THIS MY FINAL (OR INTERIM) AWARD.

Then you should say what the CLAIMANT CLAIMS and then what, if anything, the RESPONDENT COUNTERCLAIMS.

If there is any COMMON GROUND, say what it is.

Then deal with each point of claim (and counterclaim) in turn.

Briefly summarise the evidence and conclude each issue with your determination—something on the following lines:

ACCORDINGLY I HOLD THAT ...
(or FIND THAT, or even FIND AND HOLD, as most

arbitrators find difficulty in distinguishing fact and law and, to be fair, it is not always as clear-cut as you might think.)

If damages are awarded, say how much you award on that particular issue then move on to the next point of claim.

Then turn to the counterclaim and treat that in the same way, issue by issue.

The next step is to summarise what financial awards you have made, concluding with one net sum to pass from one party to the other.

Then you can say (typically):

"AND ACCORDINGLY I MAKE AND PUBLISH THIS MY FINAL AWARD—SAVE AS TO COSTS—AND I AWARD AND DIRECT THAT:
The Respondent shall pay to the Claimant, within fourteen days of this my Award, the sum of £ (words) which sum includes by way of interest the sum of £ (words) in full and final settlement of all claims and counterclaims herein, plus any VAT properly chargeable upon the Claimant by HM Customs and Excise in respect of the foregoing sum under the appropriate statutes and regulations in force at the time of publication of this award, and the Claimant shall provide to the Respondent the appropriate tax invoice in relation to the VAT so chargeable."

Finally, you must deal with the costs of the arbitration—costs of the reference and costs of the award (see Costs, p.201).

You should then state the seat of the arbitration, which is a new requirement under this Act (s.52(5)).

If counsel have been involved, say whether it is "fit for counsel" (particularly where one side only was represented by counsel) and then sign and date the award (s.52(3) and (5)). As a matter of habit I still have all of my awards witnessed by my secretary, although there is no specific requirement under the Act to do so.

Once you have signed the award you are *functus officio* and cannot change it, except under what use to be called the "slip rule"—section 57 AA '96. It is usual then to inform the parties that the award is ready for collection on payment of your final fee (having a lien on the award—s.56) or, alternatively, you draw money from that which you have put on deposit for security for your fees.

You then sit back and wait to see if either party attempts to appeal you within the 28-day period after publication of the award to the parties (s.70(3)) (although you as arbitrator will have no part in the appeals process unless the award is subsequently remitted back to you—see Post-award, p.207).

At this point, Charley dropped into the office to take Thomasina out to dinner. I explained that we had just completed our discussion on writing an award and he insisted on showing us a model that he and his pupil master use in rent review arbitration. I was happy to look through it with Thomasina but declined to comment on it, particularly as it was a totally different approach from my own and I did not wish to confuse the poor girl. However, for better or for worse, this is what Charley showed us:

EXAMPLE OF RENT REVIEW AWARD FINAL AS TO ALL MATTERS EXCEPT COSTS OF THE ARBITRATION

IN THE MATTER OF THE ARBITRATION ACT 1996 AND IN THE MATTER OF AN ARBITRATION BETWEEN C (THE CLAIMANT) AND R (THE RESPONDENT)

FIRST AWARD ON THE ISSUE OF THE RENT FINAL ON ALL MATTERS EXCEPT COSTS OF THE ARBITRATION

WHEREAS:

1. By a lease dated [date] (the "Lease") made between ... (1) and ... (2), ... (the "Property") was let for a term of ... years from [date].

2. A dispute (the "Dispute") has arisen as to the amount of the [*use the actual rent wording in the Lease*] (the "Rent") of the Property as at ... (the "Date"). Clause ... of the Lease contains an arbitration agreement to submit the Dispute to arbitration.

3. I, [full name] of [address] having given my advance consent by letter dated [date] to the Royal Institution of Chartered Surveyors was appointed by the President of the RICS Arbitrator to determine the Dispute by letter dated [date].

4. At a preliminary meeting held on [date] the parties agreed the arbitration should be conducted with a hearing which was held at [venue] on [date].

5. At an interlocutory hearing held on [date] I allowed the Respondent's application for specific discovery and made my first pre-award ruling dated [date].

6. I have read the copy of the completed stamped counterpart Lease supplied to me. I have inspected the Property and looked at the comparable properties cited to me by the parties' representatives.

7. By consent this award is on the issue of the amount of the rent with costs of the arbitration reserved if not agreed.

I HEREBY MAKE AND NOTIFY THIS MY FIRST AWARD ON THE ISSUE OF THE AMOUNT OF THE RENT FINAL ON ALL MATTERS EXCEPT COSTS OF THE ARBITRATION (the "First Award")

Example of rent review award

8. The Claimant is represented by Mr CC of Counsel (instructed by Mr ... of the Claimant Company) who called Mr CE. The Respondent is represented by Mr RA of .... I thank the parties' representatives for their careful attention and assistance given to me in this matter.

9. The Property is a ground and first floor shop used as a restaurant. Clause ... of the Lease contains the rent review provisions as to the amount of the Rent. The Lease is deemed to be incorporated on the face of this award. [*note: for the purposes of an appeal an award stands alone on its face—see* Broadgate Square plc. v. Lehman Brothers Ltd. *(1994) 1 EGLR 143 at H*].

10. The Claimant contends the Rent on the Date was £... p.a.; the Respondent £... p.a.
    More specifically:
    Mr CE's valuation (for the Claimant)
    [*set out valuation as contended for*]
    Mr RA's valuation (for the Respondent)
    [*set out as contended for*]

11. It is common ground that [*identify any relevant common ground*].

12. From the submissions and evidence I identify the issues in the Dispute are (A) [*set out issue(s) of law*]; (B) the primacy in either (i) comparable destination restaurants (introduced by Mr CE) or (ii) shop rents and a take-away restaurant rent in ... only (introduced by Mr RA).

13. The facts of the comparables are not disputed; the relevance is [*note: a "comparable" has a sufficient number of closely similar characteristics which would render the information about one property relevant to the valuation of another—see* Birmingham and Midshires Building Society v. Richard Pamplin & Co. *(1996) EGCS 3, QB*].

    For ease of reference I refer to the comparables (the "Comparables") by the comparable number as set out below.

14. Comparable 1.—[occupant] [address]
    transaction—open market letting/lease renewal/rent review ... year lease from [date]; rent £... p.a. exclusive subject to ... yearly rent reviews.
    Floor area—sales ... m^2 plus ... m^2 storage.
    Claimant's contested analysis—£... p m^2 p.a.
    Respondent's contested analysis—£... p m^2 p.a.   [*etc.*]

15. The meaning of the Rent is contained in clause ... of the Lease.

16. As to 12(A) *ante*: [*set out legal submissions including any cases referred to. Make holdings thereon, e.g. I hold that Mr CC's submission is more persuasive*].

17. As to 12(B). *ante*. Mr CE contends the best comparable evidence is that of destination restaurants, i.e. Comparables [*identify by comparable numbers*]. Mr RA contends the best evidence is shop rents and a take-away restaurant rent, i.e. Comparable [*numbers* ...]. I find that all the Comparables are relevant but I attach greatest weight to shop rents and a take-away restaurant rent relied upon by Mr RA.

18. Dealing with each of the Comparables in turn I find as follows: ... [*make findings*].

19. Having decided the issues of law, considered the analyses of the comparables, taken account of the factual evidence and weighed the opinion evidence as a matter of judgment, not as a matter of calculation, I decide that the rent per m^2 p.a. that should be applied to the Property in assessing the Rent is £... p m^2 p.a. [and the rent per m^2 that should be applied to the first floor of the Property in assessing the Rent is £... p m^2 p.a.].

20. I have not set out all the evidence and submissions but I have considered them and for the reasons I have given

21. I AWARD AND DETERMINE that the amount of the Rent of the Property was, on ... [date], £... ([words]) per year.

22. I FURTHER AWARD AND DETERMINE my total fees and expenses of this my First Award at the total sum of £... (words) including VAT in the amount of £...

23. I FURTHER AWARD AND DETERMINE that I reserve to my further award or awards my award as to the allocation of the costs of the arbitration and the recoverable costs of the arbitration if not agreed. As to all other matters this is my final award.

MADE AND NOTIFIED THIS —— DAY OF —— 19—
AT ——

ARBITRATOR
In the presence of [witness]

Notes as to reasons:

Section 52(4) requires all awards to contain reasons unless the parties have agreed otherwise.

A reasoned award should set out the arbitrator's findings (on issues of fact) and holdings (on issues of law) (mixed findings and holdings on some issues) and conclusions based upon those findings/holdings with sufficient clarity for a court to determine what those conclusions actually were to enable a court to consider any question of law arising out of the award.

Reasons include findings of fact which are material to an issue of law. However, reasons are the findings of fact upon which the argument of law will be based, not the grounds upon which the arbitrator has arrived at the findings of fact.

Reasons should include all matters upon which a party places significant reliance even if the contention is rejected.

It is an error of law to arrive at a conclusion which no reasonable arbitrator could, on the evidence, have arrived at.

If a party asked "why has the arbitrator come to this conclusion?", the award itself should provide the answer. An award is not akin to a summing up before a jury nor a judgment by a Judge; the court would be likely to reject any suggestion that everything that was said in evidence had to be dealt with and summarised in the award.

CHAPTER 12

COSTS*

The last matter with which the arbitrator has to deal in his award is costs; that is, if the parties have requested him to do so. Sometimes, particularly in the smaller disputes, the arbitrator will deal with costs in the same award as the substantive issues.

In the larger disputes, and commonly in those where the parties are legally represented, he will often be requested to deal with costs separately. This means that the arbitrator will publish his award on the substantive issues and then receive written submissions on costs following publication of this award.

In some cases, especially where counsel is involved, a short oral hearing is requested following exchange of written submissions. This is because costs can assume a very important element of an action. Indeed, in some protracted cases, parties in effect just end up fighting over costs.

If an arbitrator finds himself dealing with costs in the same award as the substantive issues, that is, where the parties, or their representatives, make their submissions—commonly orally—at the conclusion of the substantive hearing, it may be necessary for him to be given a sealed envelope to ensure that he takes into account any offers to settle which may have been made by either party (see p.68). If costs are the subject of a separate award then, following publication of his award on the substantive issues, details of any offers can be, or rather should be, openly disclosed to the arbitrator.

So remember, I said, all we are deciding now is *who* shall pay what costs, not the amount of those costs.

---

* See pp.68 and 77 and p.208, Determination Of The Parties' Costs.

WHAT COSTS?

So what costs are we talking about? asked Thomasina.

Prior to AA '96 there were two distinct costs with which the arbitrator had to deal, I said:

(i) Costs of the reference, and
(ii) Costs of the award.

Costs of the reference have been defined as the costs, other than costs of the award, incurred by the party in whose favour the order as to costs is made, and costs of the award as consisting of the fees of the arbitrator, together with any expenses that he may reasonably have incurred.

Such expenses may include room hire, costs of a transcript (although my advice is always to get the parties to deal with these costs), and fees of technical or legal assessors who may have assisted the arbitrator.

A party's costs of the reference cover all costs properly incurred by that party in connection with that reference including, *inter alia*, legal costs; the costs of preparing evidence, making submissions, and the fees and expenses of expert witnesses. These costs will normally start to run from the date when a party seeks to get the other party to concur in the appointment of an arbitrator.

In discussing this with Thomasina I suggested that she should read what Professor Robert Merkin had to say (the author of *Arbitration Act 1996—An Annotated Guide*):

"The distinction between these two classes of costs will normally be of importance only if the arbitrators make different awards for each (thus it is not uncommon for lay arbitrators to award that the parties are to bear their own costs of the reference but are to share equally the costs of the award...
[Author's note: To my knowledge this is not common in construction arbitrations].
... There is no distinction between the costs of the award and the costs of the reference as regards the scope, exercise and review of the general duty of the arbitrators to make an award as to costs...
... if the award does not keep the two types of costs distinct the award may be remitted or set aside ... The modern practice is for the arbitrators to require the payment of their fee as a precondition for handing over the award, so that the necessary separation will occur automatically."

The principle is clearly defined in AA '96 (s.61):

(1) The tribunal may make an award allocating the costs of the arbitration as between the parties, subject to any agreement of the parties.
(2) Unless the parties otherwise agree, the tribunal shall award costs on the general principle that costs should follow the event except where it appears to the tribunal that in the circumstances this is not appropriate in relation to the whole or part of the costs.

Arbitrators are bound to act judicially when exercising their discretion over costs.

AA '96 (s.59(1)(a)–(c)) deals with costs under three heads as follows:

"(1) Reference ... to the costs of the arbitration are
    (a) the arbitrators' fees and expenses,
    (b) the fees and expenses of any arbitral institution concerned, and
    (c) the legal or other costs of the parties.
(2) Any such reference includes the costs of or incidental to any proceedings to determine the amount of the recoverable costs of the arbitration (see section 63)."

When may it be appropriate for costs not to follow the event? asked Thomasina. When the arbitrator would then be making what is called an "unusual award as to costs", I said.

The following circumstances have been suggested as reasonable grounds for making such an award:

- Gross exaggeration of the claim, but the mere fact that the successful party has not recovered all that he claimed does not compel the arbitrator to disallow some or all of his costs.
- Unsatisfactory conduct by a party in the course of arbitration or unreasonable or obstructive conduct which has protracted the proceedings or increased the costs by the other party.
- Failure by the successful party on an issue or issues on which a large amount of time was spent.
- An offer by one party before or during the reference to compromise the dispute, which the other party has unreasonably failed to accept.
- Extravagance in the conduct of the hearing, e.g. the employment of an excessive number of Counsel or expert witnesses.

In making an "unusual award as to costs", therefore, the arbitrator must exercise his discretion judicially, i.e. he must have good reason for exercising his discretion in the way he did, and in such a case the arbitrator should sensibly state his reasons. It is plainly unsatisfactory that the court should be left to speculate what the arbitrator's motives might have been, I said.

What happens where there is a claim and a counterclaim? said Thomasina. These should normally be treated as two different actions, I said, and the arbitrator should first ascertain what cost items go with which action and apportion any costs involved in both. This general rule will not apply where the counterclaim is merely a "set off", or where the issues in the claim and in the counterclaim interlocked on basically the same set of facts.

I told Thomasina that I was not proposing to go into this aspect of cost at any greater depth at this stage, as there is quite a lot of authority on the subject and it is a complexity with which she need not concern herself in this general overview.

Finally, I thought that we should look at some typical clauses in an award where the parties have requested the arbitrator not to deal with costs; these might read as follows, I said:

Costs of the reference

Both Counsel have requested me to publish a Final Award—Save as to Costs.

In the event if costs cannot be agreed I shall determine them myself, and on being requested to do so, I will give directions concerning the making of written submissions on costs and a timetable for the submissions. Following determination of this issue I will publish a FINAL AWARD—ON COSTS—SAVE AS TO THE SETTLEMENT OF COSTS.

For the avoidance of doubt concerning any Costs Orders given during the reference, such orders are confirmed herewith and deemed to be incorporated in this Award.

Costs of the award

The Costs of the Award which I determine at £1175.00 (One thousand, one hundred & Seventy Five Pounds) which sum includes £175.00 (One Hundred and Seventy Five Pounds) by way of value added tax, are the joint and several liability of both parties. The ultimate liability for paying these costs will be determined in my FINAL AWARD—ON COSTS, referred to above.

If either party shall have paid, in respect of these costs, a sum greater than that which I direct in the said FINAL AWARD—ON COSTS, it is ordered to reimburse the other party forthwith.

CHAPTER 13

AGREED AWARD ON SETTLEMENT

More often than not, I told Thomasina, the parties settle their dispute before it reaches a hearing, or a determination by the arbitrator, if it is a "documents only" arbitration.

When this happens, the parties usually inform the arbitrator that they have settled on terms. Sometimes they communicate those terms to the arbitrator and at other times not. Generally, though, the parties will ask the arbitrator to incorporate those terms into what is now known as an agreed award (previously called a consent award).

The Act says that the arbitrator shall terminate the substantive proceedings (s.51(2)). Presumably if he publishes an agreed award that will have the desired effect; if he is not asked to publish such an award then he needs formally to write to the parties to the effect that the proceedings are terminated. Even if there is an award it is probably better to include something on the following lines:

"AND WHEREAS I, the said THOMASINA NASTASIA TYRO, having considered and approved the Terms of Settlement DO HEREBY ADOPT THEM and deem it appropriate to issue a Final Award and, for the avoidance of doubt, HEREBY terminate the substantive proceedings thus disposing of all matters referred to me in this dispute as set out below."

When the parties send the terms to the arbitrator it is for him to decide whether or not to incorporate these precise terms into an agreed award. The reason discretion is given to him, I said, is in case there is something in the terms with which he does not agree. This does not mean that he may in any way renegotiate the terms agreed between the parties, but more that he can resist making an award if, for example, the terms are ambiguous, unclear or contradictory, or he believes that there may well be something in the terms which is objectionable, e.g. an arrangement to defraud the tax authorities. Similarly, matters may be included which cannot properly form the subject of arbitration, for example a declaration concerning the marital status of one of the parties.

For all of these reasons, the arbitrator has the power of veto, sometimes not fully understood by the parties.

Having said that, I told Thomasina, I usually try to accommodate the parties. If there is any aspect of the terms which I find confusing or ambiguous I will usually respectfully point this out to the parties or their representatives. If they then insist, as frequently happens, that the terms are non-negotiable then, provided the point about which I am concerned is not substantially objectionable, I will publish my award, making it clear that I do so in the terms presented to me by the parties and not necessarily adopted by me, as they would be if I wholly approved of them.

The beauty of incorporating the parties' terms into an agreed award is that it is then capable of enforcement as a judgment of the court in the same way as any other award would be (s.51(3)).

CHAPTER 14

POST-AWARD

While you might think that, having published your award, you were finished with this dispute, I said, there are, in fact, one or two loose ends which may require your attention, even though you are what is known as *functus officio*, i.e. no longer having any official function.

CORRECTING ERRORS IN THE AWARD

I am sure, I said, knowing me, that you can appreciate there are occasions when, however careful one has been, errors creep into the award. Basically, what I have in mind are typographical errors, the transposition of figures, errors in a computation or referring to the claimant when you really meant to refer to the respondent—what are known in the Act as accidental slips or omissions.

AA '96 recognises that arbitrators are as fallible as any other human being, I said, and as such makes provision for an arbitrator to correct these types of errors, as well as including a new power to explain or amend a particular aspect of any award where the meaning is unclear (s.57).

The other thing that the Act provides for, I said, is to allow an arbitrator to remedy a fundamental oversight, i.e. where he has omitted to deal with a particular issue. In such a case, the arbitrator will have to make an additional award (s.57(3)(b)).

Although the arbitrator is in a position to correct his award or to publish an additional award on his own initiative, or on the application of one of the parties, he should only do so after having given the parties the opportunity of commenting on the proposed amendment or additional award—an observance of one of the rules of natural justice, right to the very end, I observed to Thomasina.

DETERMINATION OF THE PARTIES' COSTS (see p.201)

The next thing that you are likely to be involved in is a determination of the winning party's costs, I said. You will have said in your award that those "costs are to be determined by me if not agreed" and, more often than not, the parties cannot agree and they come back to you some weeks later to ask you to determine the winning party's costs.

Before AA '96, much of this *taxation* (as it used to be called) was carried out by a taxing master of the High Court, although personally I was always prepared to tax or settle the parties' costs for any of my references. AA '96 clearly gives the arbitrator discretion to determine the winning party's recoverable costs or, if he does not wish to do so, either party may apply to the court to decide how such costs should be determined (s.63).

The thought of carrying out this final task sends many arbitrators into a flat spin, I said. Basically, it is because *taxation*, as carried out by a taxing master, is governed by its own peculiar set of rules—laid down by the *White Book*.

What arbitrators must remember, I said, is that *they* are not bound by the *White Book* and therefore can take any reasonable approach to the determination of these recoverable costs, provided they tell the parties how they intend to carry out this exercise.

In my case I specify that I will determine these costs on a "reasonable costs, reasonably incurred, commercial man basis". I usually make clear that I am prepared to use the solicitor's bill to his client as a starting point, provided that I am able to identify what was being done by whom and when and how long they spent on it, and at what cost.

I realise, I said to Thomasina, that I am over-simplifying this exercise but, for the purposes of our discussion, that's as far as I'm prepared to go, at this stage. All I will say is that, of course, I issue a comprehensive Order for Directions, making it clear what procedure the parties are to follow and what it is I want from them.

APPEALS TO THE COURT (see p.177)

There are a number of very limited grounds on which a disgruntled party can challenge your award following publication, I told Thomasina. The first of these is a challenge to the arbitrator's substantive jurisdiction (s.67). Having determined the matter, the court can either confirm the award, vary it or set it aside in whole or in part.

The next possible ground of appeal is one on a point of law (s.69), provided it is brought, basically, within 28 days of the date of the award (s.70(3)). There are very limited grounds for appeal. Guidelines are laid down in the Act which perhaps can be summarised as follows:

(a) in one-off cases (that is, not involving a standard contract), leave to appeal will normally only be granted if the arbitrator is obviously wrong;
(b) in other cases leave to appeal is more freely available where there is a strong *prima facie* case that the arbitrator is wrong and, in addition, the resolution of the point would add to the clarity and certainty of the law.

Even then such an appeal may only be mounted with the consent of all the other parties or with the leave of the court. In addition to the options open to the court set out above, the court could remit the award to the arbitrator, in whole or in part, for his reconsideration in the light of their determination.

You will recall that we discussed reasons and reasoned awards earlier, I said to Thomasina (see p.74). Well, if an arbitrator has not given any reasons or does not give reasons in sufficient detail to enable the court properly to consider an appeal, the court may order the arbitrator to state, or give more, reasons (s.70(4)).

Another ground for the court remitting the award back to the arbitrator could be where he has failed to deal with costs, which the Act makes him bound to do (s.63(4)). (See pp.68, 77, 201 and 208.)

Finally, the *bête noire* of all arbitrators, *serious irregularity* (or what used to be called *misconduct*). This is the provision in the Act where the award can be challenged on a number of serious but limited grounds: in summary, for serious irregularity affecting the arbitrator, the proceedings or the award. Even under this head it is possible for the court to remit the award, in whole or in part, to the arbitrator for reconsideration, clearly depending upon the nature and seriousness of the irregularity.

It is worthy of note that there is a presumption in favour of remission rather than setting aside unless the court is satisfied that it would be inappropriate to remit (s.68(3)(c)).

Well, that's about it, I said. I've gone into far more detail than I had intended when we started this discussion, but somehow, in order to give you a fair idea of the total scope of what you might be getting into, I felt I had little choice.

I'm immensely grateful to you, godfather, said Thomasina. I really think, after what I've heard, that arbitration is something that I would derive a great deal of satisfaction from.

CHAPTER 15

OTHER FORMS OF DISPUTE RESOLUTION

I almost forgot, I said. When we embarked on this exercise I promised that before we finished I would touch very briefly on the other forms of dispute resolution—apart from litigation, that is.

What are these alternatives? I asked Thomasina. She looked blank so I suggested the following list:

- Negotiation
- Mediation
- Conciliation
- Capitulation.

Before we look at those in detail, I said, a little of the background to this search for the holy grail of dispute resolution.

ALTERNATIVE DISPUTE RESOLUTION (ADR)

ADR, imported from the United States, is currently enjoying a vogue in this country for the very reason that the other alternatives are allegedly so expensive. However, on a day-by-day comparison, ADR *can be* (but I stress need not be) as expensive, if not more so, than arbitration (but, of course, should occupy far fewer days). In the end, though, the cost of even those few days may be entirely wasted and valuable time lost.

There are several forms of ADR, but the main ones are conciliation and mediation. Mediation is the intervention, by invitation of the parties, of an independent third party in the dispute, who, by shuffling back and forth between the parties in a series of meetings, attempts to draw them towards a settlement. Conciliation is similar, but far less interventionist.

Clearly, if it works, it inevitably means a compromise with nobody winning; it is a horse deal, with the most powerful party probably compromising less than the other.

In considering ADR, the distinction between it and litigation/arbitration should be borne in mind. Quite simply the latter sets out to achieve a fair result in accordance with law and justice, while ADR specifically does not. (Although, I reminded Thomasina, since the enactment of the AA '96 there is the possibility of an equitable solution, by agreement of the parties, which is not governed by any substantive law.)

Of course, negotiation is the best form of dispute resolution and is still the most cost effective of all the alternatives.

Mediation, or indeed negotiation *per se*, is what any sensible organisation will try off its own bat, without the intervention of a highly paid third party, before resorting to other forms of dispute resolution. As over 80 per cent of all such cases settle in the end, why not negotiate *yourself* to start with and save yourself a great deal of aggravation and money!

It is said, and I agree, that there is little difference between ADR and negotiation—ADR is merely a more costly and more sophisticated form of negotiation which employs the, not inexpensive, services of a third party facilitator.

One recent report suggests that disputes under £500,000 would suit mediation. Why it should say that, I am not clear. To my mind the most cost-effective form of cost resolution depends entirely on the nature and complexity of the dispute, not on the amount in dispute.

So let us put a little more flesh on some of these alternatives, I said.

CAPITULATION

We will take the last category first.

You may laugh, Thomasina, I said, at my including capitulation, but this is happening more and more in today's climate. Parties simply cannot afford to lay out the costs in order to pursue any of the other alternatives, particularly in the smaller disputes where the costs will almost certainly exceed the amount in dispute. Also bear in mind that the successful litigant *never* receives all of his costs, even on those very rare occasions when he may be awarded indemnity costs (or its equivalent). Not only will he not recover all the money he has laid out but, in addition, he is unlikely to recover the cost of his own, or other senior management, time devoted to the case. In a small business this is not only his hourly cost to that business but the loss of opportunity to generate profit from his input.

Of course, these remarks are equally pertinent to any of the other three listed methods of resolution, and more so to litigation and arbitration.

If a party will not, or cannot, afford to capitulate, it has to resort to one of the other forms of dispute resolution I have listed, assuming, that is, that it does not go straight to arbitration or litigation.

We will look at each of these briefly in turn, I said.

NEGOTIATION

Clearly this is by far the most sensible and most common form of dispute resolution; something that most senior managers have practised throughout their professional careers. For all the above reasons, it is the most highly recommended. It has all the advantages, and, concerning cost and time, virtually none of the disadvantages, of the other forms. It also has the added merit of retaining goodwill where there is an ongoing, or a potentially ongoing, business relationship which, in most commercial disputes, can be an important factor.

MEDIATION/CONCILIATION

I shall deal with these two together, as they form the core of what is the fast-growing US-imported latest fashion in this field, ADR. (I shall, for this purpose, ignore the third form—the mini-trial.)

Mediation is, as I have already said, the intervention, by invitation of the parties, of an independent third party in the dispute, who, by shuffling between them in a series of individual meetings, attempts to draw them towards a settlement.

Conciliation, on the other hand, is similar but less interventionist.

Disadvantages of mediation/conciliation

- No guarantee of a successful outcome or, indeed, of any resolution;
- much time and money can be wasted on an abortive mediation/conciliation attempt;
- does not lend itself to complex disputes such as occur in construction;
- outcome is non-binding and only enforceable through suing on the contract—back where you started!;
- you might find yourself statute barred if ADR consumes too much time.

Despite what one is told, I said, ADR is not cheap. If lawyers and experts are involved, which they frequently are in the preparation and even the negotiation of the final settlement under ADR, costs per day can be considerably more than the daily cost of a typical arbitration on the same dispute.

The difficulty with mediation is that, in order to work, the parties have very carefully to prepare their ground. This means that they must have gone sufficiently through the discovery process to know the case against them and they will also need experts' reports, witness proofs, etc. When you get that far you have spent quite a lot of money, I told Thomasina.

A survey carried out in 1996 by an MSc student at the South Bank University came up with a cost/claim ratio of 1/9 for ADR compared with 1/10 for arbitration and 1/3 for litigation, putting arbitration in a very good light against ADR when you consider that you get a final and binding decision in arbitration.

The one perceived advantage of ADR over sensible negotiation between senior principals is that neither side is seen to make a first move towards settlement, which some interpret as a sign of weakness.

The whole point about ADR is that it is a question of "horses for courses". It certainly works in some situations and is particularly helpful where multi-parties are involved and if there is a strong desire, by all concerned, to come to some sort of settlement. On the other hand, if ADR is used for the wrong type of dispute, the acronym can well stand for Another Disastrous Result!

ADJUDICATION

Although adjudication is not arbitration, it is an option open to all commercial disputants, so I told Thomasina that it would be remiss of me if I were not to mention it in relation to building disputes in view of the Housing Grants Construction and Regeneration Act 1996 (the "Construction Act").

Adjudication itself is not new. It has been available in the construction industry, in certain standard forms of main and sub-contracts, since 1976. However, in its previous incarnations it was used for limited disputes. This may have been for single issues, such as set off, or on a limited list of issues stated in the contract.

In his final report in 1994 on the construction industry, *Constructing the Team*, Sir Michael Latham recommended that adjudication become the first tier of any dispute resolution system.

The Latham Report made the following provisions and recommendations:

"9.1 'During the past 50 years much of the United States construction environment has been degraded from one of a positive relationship between all members of the project team to a contest consumed in fault-finding and defensiveness which results in litigation. The industry has become extremely adversarial and we are paying the price ... If the construction industry is to become less adversarial, we must re-examine the construction process, particularly the relationship between contractor/subcontractor. A positive alliance of these parties constitutes an indispensable link to a successful project ... Disputes will continue as long as people fail to trust one another.' (Newsletter from 'The Dispute Avoidance and Resolution Task Force' (Dart), Washington D.C., February 1994.)

9.2 The UK construction industry is not alone in having adversarial attitudes. But the United States has taken positive steps to try to reduce them, with the growth of Alternative Dispute Resolution (ADR). The debate over adjudication, conciliation/mediation and arbitration has been very strong throughout this Review. There has been growing consensus over the action needed.

9.3 The best solution is to avoid disputes. If procedures relating to procurement and tendering are improved, the causes of conflict will be reduced. If a contract document is adopted which places the emphasis on teamwork and partnership to solve problems, that is another major step. The prepricing of variations is also important.

9.4 Nevertheless disputes may arise, despite everyone's best efforts to avoid them. A contract form with a built in adjudication process provides a clear route. If a dispute cannot be resolved first by the parties themselves in good faith, it is referred to the adjudicator for decision. Such a system must become the key to settling disputes in the construction industry. Separate adjudication is not currently provided for within JCT 80. The architect has the specific role of contract administrator there and is under a professional duty to act impartially as between employer and contractor. This was considered at length by a working party which reported to the Joint Contracts Tribunal in 1993. It made proposals for clauses in the contract providing for mediation and/or adjudication. It spelt out how those clauses should work, and what form of disputes they should include. Other than lack of agreement within the JCT, there has been nothing to prevent the introduction of such procedures within JCT 80 already.

9.5 If the NEC becomes normal construction contract documentation, its procedures for adjudication will be followed, though they may require some amendments. But adjudication should be incorporated forthwith within the JCT family as a whole. (Regarding the JCT Minor Works Form, under which work tends to be fairly quickly carried out, the Tribunal may prefer to incorporate a similar conciliation procedure to that in the ICE Minor Works Form, though there is no inherent reason why adjudication should not be used for any size of contract.) There should be no restriction on the issues to be placed before the adjudicator for decision, and no specified 'cooling off period' before the adjudicator can be called in. The adjudicator should be named in the contract before work starts but called in when necessary. The adjudicator must be neutral. If agreement cannot be reached by the parties themselves on a name or names an appointment should be made by the Presidents of one of the appropriate professional bodies. Either party to a dispute should have the right to ask for adjudication. As well as dealing with disputes between clients and main contractors, the contract documents must specify that the adjudicator must have equal scope to determine disputes between contractors and sub-contractors, and between subcontractors and sub-subcontractors. Jurisdiction on subcontract issues should not be limited to disputes over set off. It should encompass any matter which can also be within the scope of resolution under the main contract. (In many cases, disputes between clients and main contractors also involve subcontractors.) The adjudicator's fee should initially be the responsibility of the party calling in the adjudicator, but the adjudicator should subsequently apportion it as appropriate. Both main contractors and subcontractors have pressed hard for such a system to be standard procedure for dispute resolution. They should now seek to make it effective, in a spirit of teamwork.

9.6 It is crucial that adjudication decisions should be implemented at once. Mr Roger Knowles, Chairman of James R Knowles, Construction Consultants, writes
'A well drafted disputes procedure involving adjudicators and

Adjudication

arbitrators operating in an unrestricted manner will help disputes to be resolved quickly and inexpensively. For disputes settled by these methods, appeals and reference to the High Court should not be permitted under any circumstances, as it is the constant spectre of appeal which conditions the manner in which many arbitrations are conducted and which has emasculated the whole process'. (Paper by Mr Knowles, April 1994.)

9.7 I have considered this proposal. It has also been made by others, who have drawn specific attention to the role of the expert under IChemE conditions. It is correct that the authority of the adjudicator/expert must be upheld, and that the decisions should be implemented at once. Such published experience as exists of adjudication—and it does not seem very extensive at main contract level, because the possibility of the system being used appears to induce the parties to reach their own settlement without recourse to it—suggests that it is successful in reducing disputes without further appeal or litigation. But it would be difficult to deny a party which feels totally aggrieved by an adjudicator's decision any opportunity to appeal either to the courts or arbitration. I doubt whether such a restriction would be enforceable. The SEACC system, which generally defers access to the courts until after acceptance, allows such an earlier reference to the courts in certain specified and limited circumstances. However:
   1. The adjudication result must be implemented at once, even if it is subsequently overturned by the courts or an arbitrator after practical completion. If the award of the adjudicator involves payment, it must be made at once. Placing the money in the hands of an impartial stakeholder should only be permitted with the specific agreement of all the parties in the dispute, or if the adjudicator (exceptionally) so directs.
   2. The courts (unless there is some exceptional and immediate issue of law which must be brought in front of a Judge/Official Referee at once) should only be approached as a last resort and after practical completion of the contract."

Recommendations 26.1–26.5—Adjudication:

"9.14 I have already recommended that a system of adjudication should be introduced within all the Standard Forms of Contract (except where comparable arrangements already exist for mediation or conciliation) and that this should be underpinned by legislation. I also recommend that:
   1. There should be no restrictions on the issues capable of being referred to the adjudicator, conciliator or mediator, either in the main contract or subcontract documentation.
   2. The award of the adjudicator should be implemented immediately. The use of stake holders should only be permitted if both parties agree or if the adjudicator so directs.
   3. Any appeals to arbitration or the courts should be after prac-

tical completion, and should not be permitted to delay the implementation of the award, unless an immediate and exceptional issue arises for the courts or as in the circumstances described in (4).
4. Resort to the courts should be immediately available if a party refuses to implement the award of an adjudicator. In such circumstances, the courts may wish to support the system of adjudication by agreeing to expedited procedures for interim payments.
5. Training procedures should be devised for adjudicators. A Code of Practice should also be drawn up under the auspices of the proposed Implementation Forum."

Part II of the Construction Act contains the enactment of the Latham recommendations on adjudication and payment. The adjudication provisions were being prepared at the same time as the AA '96. Two separate government departments were responsible for the respective pieces of legislation. There were allegations in the construction industry press that there was somewhat of a mismatch between the two statutes.

The themes of the AA '96 are party autonomy and that arbitration is a wholly consensual process. The legislation on adjudication does not consider party autonomy at all and adjudication is not consensual. The right to take a dispute to adjudication at any time is compulsory. The Construction Act defines construction contracts and gives the minimum criteria that every construction contract must contain in respect of adjudication.

These criteria are contained in s.108 of this Act and are as follows:

"(2) The Contract shall—
(a) enable a party to give notice at any time of his intention to refer a dispute to adjudication;
(b) provide a timetable with the object of securing the appointment of the adjudicator and referral of the dispute to him within 7 days of such notice;
(c) require the adjudicator to reach a decision within 28 days of referral or such longer period as is agreed by the parties after the dispute has been referred;
(d) allow the adjudicator to extend the period of 28 days by up to 14 days, with the consent of the party by whom the dispute was referred;
(e) impose a duty on the adjudicator to act impartially; and
(f) enable the adjudicator to take the initiative in ascertaining the facts and the law.

Adjudication 219

(3) The contract shall provide that the decision of the adjudicator is binding until the dispute is finally determined by legal proceedings, by arbitration (if the contract provides for arbitration or the parties otherwise agree to arbitration) or by agreement. The parties may agree to accept the decision of the adjudicator as finally determining the dispute.

(4) The contract shall also provide that the adjudicator is not liable for anything done or omitted in the discharge or purported discharge of his functions as adjudicator unless the act or omission is in bad faith, and that any employee or agent of the adjudicator is similarly protected from liability."

If the construction contract fails to provide all eight of the criteria set out in s.108 of the Construction Act, there is secondary legislation which implies terms into all construction contracts in any event. This secondary legislation is called the *Scheme for Construction Contracts (England and Wales) Regulations 1998*.

The Scheme covers the minimum criteria set out in the Act. It also covers a number of practical criteria similar to those matters found in sets of arbitration Rules. The 26 regulations which cover adjudication set out such matters as appointment; resignation of the adjudicator; powers of the adjudicator; joinder; the decision; enforcement and adjudicators' fees.

The legislation became operative on 1st May 1998. There has been considerable debate in the industry on whether in practice adjudication will work and what its effect will be on arbitration. Lord Saville made the following statement in the Foreword to a recent book on arbitration:

"What has also given rise to some criticism is the interrelationship between arbitration and adjudication. I'm the first to accept that this is a very important topic indeed, but to my mind criticism of the Arbitration Act is misplaced. This Act can work well and effectively with adjudication, if the latter is properly considered and worked out. Great efforts are being made to develop adjudication and I'm hopeful that in the future these two quite different concepts will be able to work properly together."

Well, my dear Thomasina, I said, here endeth the lesson. We have pretty well exhausted the topic, and if you don't know enough about the workings of arbitration after all this time then I have failed in my task.

Thank you so much, godfather, she replied, for taking so much trouble and giving up so much of your valuable time. Certainly I now have a jolly good idea of what arbitration is all about. I shall have to give very careful thought to what it means in terms of commitment and time if I decide to attempt to qualify as an arbitrator. I shall get in touch with the Chartered Institute of Arbitrators and find out what the first move is.

Well, that is the entry course, I said, but they will tell you all about that. Bless you and good luck if you decide to go ahead, I said.

INDEX

ABTA, and holiday disputes, 10
ACAS (Arbitration and Conciliation Service), 5
Accommodation/venue, full procedure with Hearing, 45–46, 70
Ad hoc agreements, 11
Adjudication, 215–220
ADR (alternative dispute resolution), 5, 211–212, 213, 214, 215
Advantages of arbitration
  confidentiality, 17
  costs, 17
  flexibility, 18
  speed, 17
Adversarial or inquisitorial process?, 169–172
Advocates' submissions
  full procedure with Hearing, 47, 73
  Order for Directions, 96
Agenda, Preliminary Meeting, 22, 31–88
  Agreement of Common Ground, 49, 78–79
  appointment of arbitrator, 33–34, 50–51
  Arbitrator's Terms and Conditions, 14, 49, 79–86
  commencement of arbitration, 34, 52–53
  costs, 48, 77–78
  exclusion agreement, 48, 76
  identification of items in dispute, 34, 53–55
  inspection, 49, 78
  insurance, 49, 86–87
  introductions, 33, 50
  issues, 36, 61

Agenda, Preliminary Meeting—*cont.*
  joinder/consolidation, 36, 61
  jurisdiction, 34, 51–52
  reasoned award, 47–48, 74–76
  rent review arbitrations, 114–116
  representation, 47, 73–74
  seat and applicable law, 34, 52
  see also Powers of arbitrator; Proceedings
Agreed award on settlement, 205–206
Agreement of parties, powers of arbitrator, 58
Agricultural Holdings Act 1986, 103, 133–134
Appeals, 9, 18, 209–210
Applicable law
  agenda, Preliminary Meeting, 34, 52
  Order for Directions, Preliminary Meeting, 90
Appointment of arbitrator, 11–17, 20, 24
  agenda, Preliminary Meeting, 33–34, 50–51
  Order for Directions, Preliminary Meeting, 90, 99
Appointments—nominated or consensual, Rent Review Arbitrations, 122
Arbitration Act 1996 (AA '96)
  adjudication, 218
  appeals, 209
  and arbitrator, 170
  awards, 191, 194, 196
    errors in, 207
  costs, 203
  court's role, 177, 178
  powers of arbitrator, 8–9

Index

Arbitration Act 1996—*cont.*
  see also Agenda, Preliminary
    Meeting; Interlocutory
    period/directions; Order for
    Directions; Rent Review
    Arbitrations
Arbitration agreements, 6, 7, 10
  appointment of arbitrator, 16
  in writing, 8, 51
Arbitration clauses, 6–7
Arbitrators
  adversarial or inquisitorial process?,
    169–172
  immunity of, 174–175
  resignation, 173
  termination, 174
  use of own expertise, 172–173
  see also Appointment of arbitrator;
    Fees; Terms and Conditions
Awards
  agreed on settlement, 205–206
  analysis of, 188–190
  appeals against, 18
  correcting errors in, 207
  costs of, 202, 204
  Declaratory: powers of arbitrator,
    35, 58
  drafting, 190
  essentials of valid, 190–191
  final, 191, 193, 194
  interim, 193
  Order for Directions, Preliminary
    Meeting, 96
  provisional: interlocutory directions,
    167
  reasoned, 190
    agenda, Preliminary Meeting,
      47–48, 74–76
  reasons: award example, 199
  Rent Review Arbitrations
    example, 196–199
    reasons in, 135–137
  structure and content, 191–195
  writing of, 5–6, 187–199

Bar Council, 12
Barristers, 73
Bias of arbitrator, 12
Bingham, Sir Thomas, 135
Breach of contract, 54, 187–188

Capitulation, 212–213
Chartered Institute of Arbitrators, 12

Charterparties, 12
CIMAR (Construction Industry
  Model Arbitration Rules), 7, 33,
  50, 56
  see also "Sanctuary House Case"
Civil Evidence Act (CEA '95), 132
Commencement of arbitration
  agenda, Preliminary Meeting, 34,
    52–53
  Order for Directions, Preliminary
    Meeting, 90
Commencement of hearing, 183
Common ground, 193
  agenda, Preliminary Meeting, 49,
    78–79
  Order for Directions, Preliminary
    Meeting, 96
  statement of, 149
Common law, and powers of arbitrator, 9
Communications, Order for
  Directions, Preliminary Meeting,
  97–98
Conciliation, 211, 213–214
  ACAS, 5
Conduct of reference, Order for
  Directions, Preliminary Meeting,
  91
Confidentiality, in arbitration, 17
Consolidation, 10, 36, 61
"Construction Act" *see* Housing
  Grants Construction and
  Regeneration Act 1996
Construction contracts *see* JCT
Construction industry, 7
  see also CIMAR
Constructional issues, Rent Review
  Arbitrations, 132
Contractors and sub-contractors, 54
Contracts, 187–188, 193
  breach of contract, 54, 187–188
  Order for Directions, Preliminary
    Meeting, 90
Costs, 175, 201–204
  agenda, Preliminary Meeting, 48,
    77–78
  of arbitration, 17
  of arbitrator, 25
  awards, 191, 194, 202, 204
  determination of parties' costs, 208
  full procedure with Hearing, 68–69
  interlocutory directions: security for
    costs, 157–163

Costs—*cont.*
  Order for Directions, Preliminary Meeting, 96–97, 101
  of the reference, 202, 203, 204
  of winning party, 28
  see also Fees; Terms and conditions
Court of Appeal, powers of the arbitrator, 9
Courts
  appeals to, 209–210
  powers of: Order for Directions, Preliminary Meeting, 97
  role in arbitral proceedings, 177–179
Courts of Pie Powder (*pieds poudrés*), 3

Damages, quantum of, 188–190
Declaratory award, powers of arbitrator, 35, 58
Default of a party, powers of arbitrator, 35, 58
Defences, Rent Review Arbitrations, 129
Definitions of arbitration, 5, 8
Denning, Lord, 75–76, 166, 191–193
Documents
  disclosure of
    full procedure with Hearing, 43–44, 67
    Order for Directions, 93–94
  service of: full procedure with Hearing, 44
"Documents only" procedure, 25
  agenda: Preliminary Meeting, 22, 37–38, 57, 58, 62–63, 64
  the hearing, 182
  rent review arbitrations, 107, 112, 117–125, 132–133, 134
Duty of arbitrator: rent review arbitrations, 130

Estopped by waiver, appointment of arbitrator, 15
Evidence
  admissibility: rent review arbitrations, 132–134
  evaluating opinion evidence: rent review arbitrations, 134–135
  full procedure with Hearing, 46, 71–72
  oral, 35, 47, 56–57, 63–64, 72
  proofs of: Order for Directions, 95
  under oath, 46, 71–72
  written, 35, 56–57, 63–64

Ex aequo et bono, 9
Ex parte proceedings, interlocutory directions, 165–166
Exclusion agreement, agenda, Preliminary Meeting, 48, 76
Experts
  appointing of: powers of arbitrator, 58–59
  full procedure with Hearing, 41–43, 66–67
  Order for Directions, Preliminary Meeting, 93
  Rent Review Arbitrations, 122, 123

Fees and expenses of arbitrator, 106, 175–176
  see also Costs; Terms and conditions
Functus officio, 194, 207

Goff, Lord, 75
Hearings, 181–185
  checklist, 183
  commencement, 183
  Order for Directions, Preliminary Meeting, 94–95
  pleadings, 182
  pre-hearing review, 181
    interlocutory directions, 167–168
  submission of items in dispute, 55
  see also under Proceedings

High Court, 153
  "payments in", 68
  powers of the arbitrator, 9
  rules governing *see Supreme Court Practice*
House of Lords, powers of the arbitrator, 9
Housing Grants Construction and Regeneration Act 1996, 215, 218–219

ICE Arbitration Procedure, 7
Identify items in dispute, agenda, Preliminary Meeting, 34, 53–55
Immunity of arbitrator, 174–175
Inflation, and rent reviews, 7
Inquisitorial or adversarial process?, 169–172
Inspection, agenda, Preliminary Meeting, 49, 78

Insurance, agenda, Preliminary Meeting, 49, 86–87
Interest, award of, 57
Interlocutory directions, 140–168
  awards/partial awards, 166–167
  discovery, 163–164
  ex parte proceedings, 165–166
  extensions of time, 164
  failing to comply with arbitrator's directions, 164–165
  further and better particulars, 142–145
    alternatives to, 149–150
    disadvantages, 145–146
    failure to comply with, 146
    unless order in respect of failure to reply to, 147–148
  notices to admit facts and interrogatories, 149–155
  pre-hearing review, 167–168
  requests for further and better particulars, 142–143
  Scott Schedule, 141
  security for costs applications, 157–163
  typical Order re Notice to Admit Facts, 151–155
  typical request for interrogatories, 156
Interlocutory period, 139–168
Interrogatories, interlocutory period, 153–154, 155, 156
Interviews, 15
Introductions, agenda, Preliminary Meeting, 33, 50
Irregularity, 209–210
Issues, agenda, Preliminary Meeting, 36, 61

JCT Arbitration Rules, 7
  identifying items in dispute, 53
  joinder/consolidation, 61
  jurisdiction, 51–52
  powers of arbitrator, 57, 58, 60
  proceedings, 36, 61, 63
  "Sanctuary House Case", 19, 20–21, 22–23, 24, 26–28
JCT family of building contracts, appointment of arbitrator, 11–12
Joinder
  agenda, Preliminary Meeting, 36, 61
  powers of, 10

Jurisdiction
  of arbitrator: Agenda, Preliminary Meeting, 34, 51–52
  Order for Directions, Preliminary Meeting, 90, 100
  and powers of arbitrator, 7–8, 10

Latham Report, 215–218
Law reports/authorities, Order for Directions, 96
Law Society, appointment of arbitrator, 12
Lawyers *see* Advocates; Barristers; Solicitors
Letters
  letter following appointment, 19–29
  model letter: Rent Review Arbitrations, 103–107
Limitations, on powers of arbitrator, 9–10
Limitations Acts, 53
Litigation, and arbitration, 17–18
LMAA, 16

Mance J, 124
Maritime cases, 7
  appointment of arbitrator, 12, 16
Mediation, 211, 212, 213–214
  ACAS, 5
Model Letter: Rent Review Arbitrations, 103–107
Mustill, Lord, 3, 75, 130, 171

Negotiation, 212, 213
Northern Ireland, 52
Notice of arbitration, 50
Notices to admit facts and interrogatories, 149–155
Notification date, 21, 24

Offers to settle, 184
Oral evidence, 35, 47, 56–57, 63–64, 72
Oral hearings, Rent Review Arbitrations, 122–125
Oral submissions, 185, 201
Order for Directions
  "documents only": Rent Review Arbitrations, 119–121
  interlocutory period, 147–149, 151–152, 156, 160–163
Order for Directions, Preliminary Meeting, 22, 88, 89–101

Index

Order for Directions, Preliminary Meeting—*cont.*
  Advocates' submissions, 96
  agreed bundle, 95
  appointment, 90
  awards, 96
  commencement of arbitration, 90
  common ground, 96
  communications, 97–98
  conduct of reference, 91
  contract, 90
  costs, 96–97, 101
  counsel, 93
  court's powers, 97
  disclosure of documents, 93–94
  experts, 93
  further directions, 101
  general powers of arbitrator, 90–91, 100
  hearing, 94–95
  jurisdiction, 90, 100
  law reports/authorities, 96
  liberty to apply, 98
  parties, 89, 99
  preliminary issues, 92
  proofs of evidence, 95
  seat and applicable law, 90
  service, 92–93, 100
  timetable, 92

Partiality of arbitrator, 12
Parties
  determination of costs, 208
  Order for Directions, Preliminary Meeting, 89, 99
Peremptory Orders, 177
Perjury, 10
Pleadings
  at hearing, 182
  Rent Review Arbitrations, 116–122, 125–129
Powers of arbitrator
  agenda, Preliminary Meeting, 34–36, 55–60
    appointing experts, 58–59
    award of interest, 57
    in case of party's default, 35, 58
    declaratory award, 35, 58
    initiative of tribunal, 56
    oral or written evidence, 35, 56–57
    order provisional relief, 60
    order rectification of deed or document, 59–60

Powers of arbitrator—*cont.*
  agenda, Preliminary Meeting—*cont.*
    order specific performance of contract, 59
    order to party, 59
    recording parties' agreement, 58
  arbitration agreement, 6, 7
  common law, 9
  jurisdiction, 7–8
  limitations, 9–10
  Order for Directions, Preliminary Meeting, 90–91, 100
  statute law, 8–9
Preliminary issues, Order for Directions, Preliminary Meeting, 92
Preliminary Meeting, 12, 31–101
  Rent Review Arbitrations, 103, 105, 107, 108–116
  "Sanctuary House Case", 21, 22–23, 24, 25–27, 28
  see also Agenda, Preliminary Meeting; Order for Directions
Procedural and evidential matters, 8
Proceedings: agenda, Preliminary Meeting, 36–37, 61–62
  Documents Only, 37–38, 62–63, 64
  Full procedure with Hearing, 38–47, 63–73
    Advocates' submissions, 47, 73
    disclosure of documents, 43–44, 67
    evidence under oath, 46, 71–72
    experts, 41–43, 66–67
    Hearing bundle, 46, 70–71
    limitation on orality, 47, 72
    offers, 68–69
    Pre-Hearing Review, 45, 69
    rules of evidence, 46, 71
    Scott Schedule, 38, 64, 69
    text books/law reports, 47, 72–73
    timetable, 38–40, 64–65
    venue/accommodation, 45–46, 70
    witness statements, 40–41, 65–66
  Short procedure with Hearing, 38, 63
Provisional relief, powers of arbitrator, 60
Public policy, limitation on powers of arbitrator, 10

Quantum of damages, 188–190

Receivers, appointment of, 10
Referral of dispute, 9
Rent Review Arbitrations, 7, 12, 103–137
  appointments—nominated or consensual, 122
  arbitrator's duty, 130
  award example, 196–199
  defences, 129
  "documents only", 107, 112, 117–122, 132–133, 134
  model letter, 103–107
  oral hearings or "documents only"?, 122–125
  Order for Directions on Documents Only, 119–121
  pleadings, 116–122
  pleadings or statement of case?, 125–129
  Preliminary Meeting, 103, 105, 107
    agenda for, 114–116
    direction for, 108–112
  procedural problems, 131–135
    admissibility of evidence, 132–134
    constructional issues, 132
    evaluating opinion evidence, 134–135
    process of reasoning, 130–131
    reasons in awards, 135–137
Representation
  agenda, Preliminary Meeting, 47, 73–74
  at hearing, 183
  choice in arbitration, 18
Resignation of arbitrator, 173
RIBA (Royal Institute of British Architects), appointment of arbitrator, 12, 15
RICS (Royal Institution of Chartered Surveyors), appointment of arbitrator, 11–12, 13–14, 15, 20
RSC *see Supreme Court Practice*

"Sanctuary House Case", 19–29
  see also Agenda, Preliminary Meeting; Order for Directions
Saville, Lord, 219
Scotland, law in, 52
Scott Schedule, 170–171
  interlocutory directions, 141

Scott Schedule—*cont.*
  proceedings, 38, 64, 69
  Rent Review Arbitrations, 127
Seat and applicable law
  agenda, Preliminary Meeting, 34, 52
  Order for Directions, Preliminary Meeting, 90
Service, Order for Directions, Preliminary Meeting, 92–93, 100
"Slip rule", 194
Sole arbitrators, 16
Solicitors, 73
  appointment of arbitrator, 11
  identifying items in dispute, 53
Statement of case, Rent Review Arbitrations, 125–129
Statements, service of: full procedure with hearing, 44
Supreme Court Practice/Rules of the Supreme Court (White Book), 8, 126, 208

Technical experts, appointing of, 58–59
Technical and legal arbitrators, 16
Termination, arbitrator, 174
Terms and conditions of arbitrator, 23, 28, 175
  Agenda, Preliminary Meeting, 14, 49, 79–86
  see also Fees, Costs
Third parties
  appointment of arbitrator, 13
  jurisdiction over, 10
Timetable
  full procedure with Hearing, 38–40, 64–65
  Order for Directions, Preliminary Meeting, 92
Transfer of rights reserved by courts, 10
Tribunal, of more than one arbitrator, 16

Venue/accommodation, full procedure with Hearing, 45–46, 70
Vinava Shipping Co. Ltd v. *Finelvet AG ("The Chrysalis")*, 130, 131

White Book see Supreme Court Practice
Witnesses
  in arbitration, 17–18
  at the hearing, 184, 185

Witnesses—*cont.*
  statements
    full procedure with Hearing,
      40–41, 65–66

Witnesses—*cont.*
  statements—*cont.*
    in Rent Review Arbitrations,
      116

Special Offer—Save £148!

Arbitration Practice and Procedure: Interlocutory and Hearing Problems
SECOND EDITION

The Sanctuary House Case: An Arbitration Workbook

by D. Mark Cato MSc (Construction Law and Arbitration), FRICS, FCIArb, Registered Arbitrator

Buy both Lloyd's Commercial Law Library Titles for £200 and save a massive £148!

These two complementary titles will give you all the fact-based law and discursive information that you need for your arbitration requirements. *Arbitration Practice and Procedure: Interlocutory and Hearing Problems, Second Edition*, is an authoritative reference book to help you with legal and procedural problems. *The Sanctuary House Case* is a breath of fresh air with its unorthodox approach, detailing all stages on the arbitral process; an invaluable guide to everything that can possibly happen.

Arbitration Practice and Procedure: Interlocutory and Hearing Problems, Second Edition is the guide for practitioners in this field and has been recently completely revised in light of the Arbitration Act 1996. With its unique problem-solving approach, the first edition of this text rapidly became a standard text on Arbitration.

"The test of any work of reference is the frequency of its use. This volume will not gather dust. Most will regard it as an essential source of information."
Arbitration, Journal of the Chartered Institute of Arbitrators

"... when it comes to the solution of problems which can arise during a difficult arbitration, it is hard to think of any significant area where this book is lacking."
The Lawyer

More Problems Solved
It now provides some 600 examples of problems encountered on a daily basis by professional advisers, lawyers, arbitrators, expert witnesses and parties to arbitration. Each problem situation is described—the facts of the case and the questions to which it gives rise—and a course or courses of action suggested.

Now extensively rewritten, with all new recent case law, the author has expanded commentary and examples to reflect recent developments. The second edition includes the type of problems that arise under the Arbitration Act 1996, and is now an even richer source of valuable practical help in suggesting solutions to questions of practice and procedure.

ISBN 1 85978 150 0   Hardcover   1812pp   1997

TURN OVER TO PLACE YOUR ORDER

The Sanctuary House Case: An Arbitration Workbook

Foreword by Sir Thomas Bingham
Master of the Rolls

Endorsed by The Royal Institution of Chartered Surveyors

The Sanctuary House Case: An Arbitration Workbook is an innovative and unique practice manual. *Volume One* outlines a hypothetical situation based on real-life cases, addressing the entire arbitral process from appointment of arbitrator to award. *Volume Two* leads the practitioner through many practice suggestions and solutions, substantiated by appropriate documentation including invaluable in-depth commentary on each clause of the Arbitration Act 1996.

Extensive cross-referencing between volumes enable and encourage the reader to work through both common and complex arbitral issues. The author has succeeded in closing the gap between the theory of arbitration law, substantive law and procedural law and the practical management of the arbitral process.

"It manages to achieve the unlikely feat of presenting a full-blown construction adjudication in a thoroughly digestible form, full of human interest. This the author does with great skill, presenting many different facets of the case, starting with the project and running on to the generation of a series of both usual and unusual disputes and issues, right through the arbitration and out the other end."
Professor John Uff QC

Contents for Volumes 1 and 2 (Volume 2 gives extracts of relevant correspondence)

1 Introduction and Author's Health Warning
2 Prelude
3 The Appointment
4 The Preliminary Meeting
5 Preliminary Issues
6 Pleadings
7 The Interlocutory Period
8 Pre-Hearing Review
9 Security for Costs
10 The Hearing
11 The Award
12 Fees and how to get them paid
13 Appeals to the High Court
14 Taxation (or Settlement) of Costs
15 Enforcement
16 Epilogue

ISBN 1 85044 853 1   Hardcover   2 volumes   1492pp   1996

TURN OVER TO PLACE YOUR ORDER

PRIORITY ORDER FORM: FAX BACK TO +44 (0)171 553 1107

Please complete and return to:
Wayne Hurley, LLP Limited, 69–77 Paul Street, London, EC2A 4LQ
Telephone: +44 (0)171 553 1732 Fax: +44 (0)171 553 1107

☐ I would like to take advantage of the special offer and order __ copy(ies) of ***Arbitration Practice and Procedure: Interlocutory and Hearing Problems, Second Edition & The Sanctuary House Case: An Arbitration Workbook***
@ £200/US$340/HK$2652

☐ I would like to order __ copy(ies) of ***Arbitration Practice and Procedure: Interlocutory and Hearing Problems, Second Edition***
@ £163/US$277/HK$2161   ISBN 1 85978 150 0

☐ I would like to order __ copy(ies) of
The Sanctuary House Case: An Arbitration Workbook
@ £185/US$315/HK$2453   ISBN 1 85044 853 1

Name:_____ Company:_____

Address:_____

_____

_____

Country:_____ Postcode:_____

Job Title:_____ Nature of Business:_____

Telephone:_____ Fax:_____

PAYMENT DETAILS

Please charge my credit/charge card (delete as appropriate)

VISA   ACCESS/MASTERCARD   AMEX   EUROCARD   DINERS

Card Account Number:_____

Card Expiry Date:_____ Signature:_____

☐ Please send me a pre-payment invoice. Your supply will commence upon receipt of your payment

☐ Cheque/money order is enclosed payable to LLP Limited in £/US$/HK$

☐ Tick here if you do not want to receive direct mail from other companies

Lloyd's is the registered trade mark of the Society incorporated by the Lloyd's Act 1871 by the name of "Lloyd's".